Highways & Byways

Illustrated walks in Norfolk

By

Marion Addy

Highways and Byways illustrated walks in Norfolk by Marion Addy

First published in Great Britain in 2021.

All the walks described have public access or are permissive paths, as such they are subject to change.

The illustrative maps are a guide only and should be used in conjunction with the appropriate OS map for the area.

The author takes no responsibility for loss or damage to persons, goods or vehicles parked at the suggested location or while on the route.

ISBN 978-1-5272-8916-1

British Library Cataloguing-in-Publication-Data.

A record of this title is available from the British Library.

Printed in Cromer, Norfolk by Cheverton Printers.

Front cover: Holkham Gap.
Back cover: Buzzards at Holkham / View of Burnham Overy Tower Mill from Burnham Market

CONTENTS

Foreword

We know how very lucky we are to have such lovely walks in Norfolk. Marion Addy was born in Honing, near North Walsham, and has lived there ever since. She has walked thousands of miles throughout the county and we are very fortunate that she has been inspired to share with us a series of her favourite walks.

To find a route is one thing but, to really enjoy a walk, a walker needs interesting information about points of interest so that they can experience and understand the landscape in all its aspects. Marion's detailed descriptions of the routes should enable walkers to find their way easily but it is the carefully researched supplementary notes that bring these walks to life. Her delightful pencil and watercolour sketches show that she does not rush along the routes but takes the time to enjoy them properly, as should we.

The book is delightful and will inspire people to enjoy and appreciate the countryside by walking in it with knowledge and care.

William Cubitt

March 2021

Introduction

Norfolk is a large county of about 5,360 square kilometres, with some 600 villages and market towns. It is relatively isolated from the rest of England. The sea borders its northern and eastern edge, the once almost impenetrable Fens forms the western boundary and the rivers Little Ouse and Waveney provide a near continuous border to the south. It was first recognised as a separate area in 672, with the creation of a bishopric at North Elmham (transferred to Norwich in 1096). With the exception of the Fens, all of Norfolk has always been habitable. From about 1000 to 1600, Norfolk was the most densely populated county in England. The population was focused around the three large settlements of Norwich (which from about 1350 to 1750 was the second city of England), King's Lynn and Great Yarmouth and a number of smaller market towns, which served the rural village populations within a radius of five to ten miles. Many of the villages in the county have their origins in the Saxon period or earlier. In most, the oldest building is often the parish church. Norfolk has nearly 2,000 medieval churches, many dating from the fourteenth or fifteenth centuries, replacing earlier Saxon or Norman buildings. During the eighteenth century the Church in Norfolk went into a decline (the Diocese of Norwich was called the 'Dead See'), however, during the nineteenth century there was something of a revival, with many parish churches being 'improved' between 1850 and 1900.

The sea has always been important for Norfolk; it was the way in which many early settlers arrived in the county. As sea levels have fluctuated during glacial and interglacial periods, the North Sea basin, Doggerland, has alternated between land and sea. During periods of low sea level, it would have been possible to walk across Doggerland from what is now continental Europe. Sites at Happisburgh in Norfolk and Pakefield in Suffolk have provided the earliest evidence for human activity in Britain. The sea has also been important in terms of trade, with routes to Scandinavia and the Low Countries from ports which are active today, for example, King's Lynn and Great Yarmouth, and others which have all but disappeared, for example, Cley. Yarmouth was also an important base for the herring fishing industry. As well as providing opportunity, the sea is also a threat to the county. Rising sea levels have the potential to inundate the Fens, where most of the land is only a few metres above sea level and in some places below it. Also, Norfolk has one of the most mobile coastlines in the country. Its north and north-eastern coastline has always been subject to change caused by cliff erosion. This is partly caused by wave action and partly by groundwater. The cliffs in this section of coastline are made of boulder clay (sands and gravels), when this material is saturated it becomes unstable and can result in sections of cliff slumping down onto the beach. As the frequency of intense rainfall events increases, so the rate of coastal erosion is also likely to increase.

Agriculture has always been an important industry in Norfolk, with the soils and climate favouring arable production. Not surprisingly, Norfolk played an important part in the Agrarian Revolution through the influence of 'improvers' such as Viscount 'Turnip' Townsend at Raynham and 'Coke of Norfolk' at Holkham. Wheat has been an important crop since Roman times, to this has been added barley, sugar beet and oilseed rape, as well as more unusual crops such as lavender and sunflowers. The Fens, which were drained in the seventeenth century, is an area noted for its production of vegetables. During the eighteenth and nineteenth centuries, many of the old Medieval estates in Norfolk were amalgamated, through purchase, inheritance or marriage, so that by the 1880s, over half of Norfolk was owned by landowners with estates of over 1000 acres. The agricultural depression of the late nineteenth century and the social, political and economic changes of the twentieth century have reversed this trend, with a number of estates being reduced in size or split up and sold, often with the associated country house being demolished. In 1914, one in six farmers in the county were owner-occupiers, by the end of the century this had risen to two out of every three. The late nineteenth and early twentieth centuries saw the arrival of non-landed money in Norfolk, with many industrialists and financiers buying land and building houses, often in coastal locations, for leisure and sporting purposes.

Norfolk has also had important non-agricultural, manufacturing industries, largely centred on Norwich. Until the early nineteenth century, Norwich was, with the West Riding of Yorkshire and parts of the West Country, an important centre for textile manufacturing, particularly the worsted industry. Norwich was also an important centre for the manufacture of women's and children's shoes, insurance, the packing of starch and mustard, the production of chocolate and mineral water and the production of wire netting and wooden and steel buildings. While many of these industries have declined, the creation of the University of East Anglia, in the 1960s, has attracted growth in the High Tech and life science sectors. Tourism is another growth industry, beginning with the arrival of the railways in the late nineteenth century which brought people from the Midlands to resorts such as Yarmouth, Hunstanton and Sheringham. From the mid-twentieth century, there has been a thriving boating holiday industry, based on the Broads.

Norfolk is a county ideally suited for travel on foot; although it is not as flat as is often believed. The gently undulating landscape makes for easy walking, and what counts for hills in the county give impressive views of the surrounding landscape. The highest point in the county is the Cromer Ridge formed by terminal moraine, and is a lasting reminder of the ice sheet which once covered Norfolk. Each walk in this book is in three sections: a map, a description of the route, and points of interest which can be seen along the route. The maps are not drawn to scale. A car park is suggested from which to the start the walk (for which an OS map sheet number and grid reference or Sat Nav postcode is given), please note, in some cases, there may be a charge made for parking. The approximate length of each route is also given, as is an estimate of time taken to complete it. When purchasing a car park ticket, please ensure you allow sufficient time to complete the walk. If you are not using the suggested car park, please park responsibly, in a safe way, without causing a nuisance to other road users. When on the route please follow the Countryside Code and observe all signs and diversions you may encounter along the way. The points of interest given are not exhaustive, they are provided to give an indication of the varied history of the area. The illustrations show some of the buildings, landscapes, and flora and fauna you may encounter on your journey.

The route for each walk was researched during the Covid 19 Pandemic in 2020. While no mention is made to them in the text, many of the towns and villages through which the walks pass have pubs, cafes and restaurants, which would no doubt be delighted to receive your custom should you need refreshment en route.

Acknowledgements

This book is the product of the many decades I have spent walking in Norfolk. Firstly, I must thank all those who over the years have suggested new walks for me to try. I owe a debt of gratitude to my parents, Barbara and Herbert, for their Sunday outings to the churches, historic sites and gardens of Norfolk, which opened up a new world and fostered my interest in the landscape and history of Norfolk. I would like to thank William Cubitt for his foreword and Lucy Cubitt for reading through the book and noticing those errors I had missed. Whatever errors remain are mine and mine alone. Also, I would like to thank Mark at Chevertons.

Marion Addy
March 2021

Periodisation

Stone Age -this period in pre-history is usually divided into three periods:

Palaeolithic	900,000 -11,000BC
Mesolithic	11,000 - 4000BC
Neolithic	4000 - 2500BC
Bronze Age	2500 - 800BC
Iron Age	800BC - 43AD
Roman	43 - 410AD
Anglo Saxon	410 - 1066AD
Norman	1066 - 1154AD

Key to Maps

Road

Track/Footpath

Woodland

Settlement

Water

Railway

Marsh

Point of interest

Suggested car park

Common/Heath or Grassland

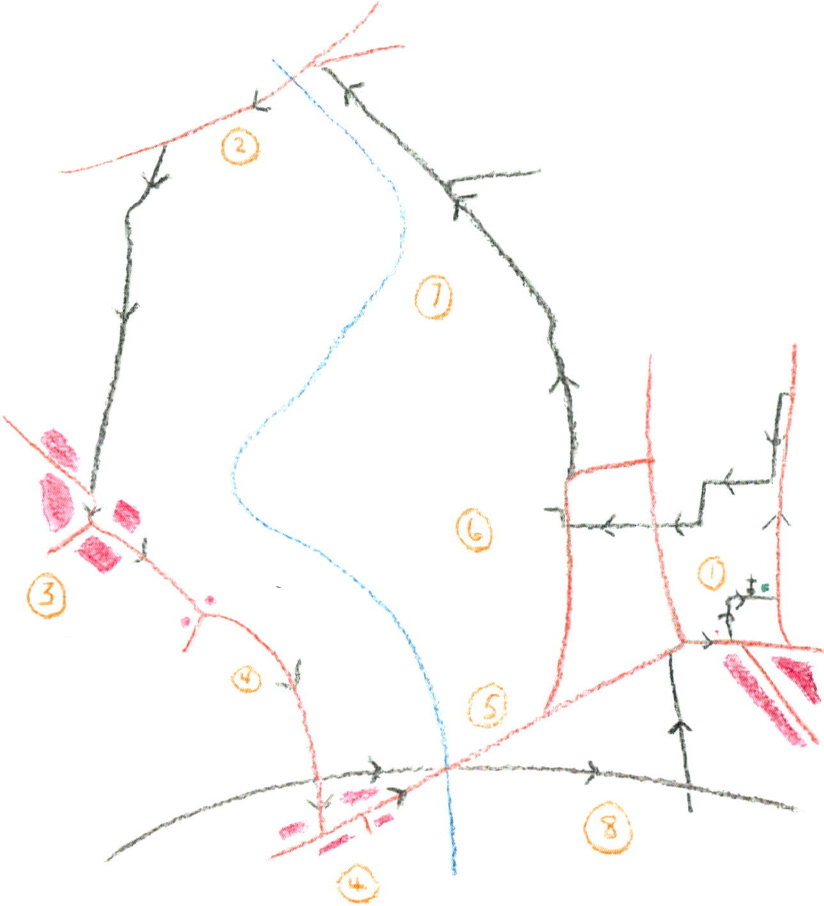
2
7
6
1
3
4
5
8
4

Walk 1: *Honing, Meeting Hill and Briggate*

Summary

This route begins in Honing and makes its way, through arable fields, to Meeting Hill and Briggate using country lanes, footpaths and rough tracks. It crosses and re-crosses the North Walsham and Dilham Canal. Some of the paths are uneven and there are some moderate gradients on the route.

The Route

Distance: 6¼ miles.
Time: 2½/3 hours.
Suggested car park: St. Peter and St. Paul's Church, Honing NR28 9QW.
TG 3262 2800
Map Sheet: OS Explorer 0L40
Alternative car parking: Honing Station

1. Turn left out of the car park and walk to the field gateway. Ignoring the footpath to the right, turn left into the field and follow the footpath towards the beech hedge.

2. At the beech hedge, turn right and continue along the path. At the end of the hedge, turn left (ignoring the track to the right signed 'Private'). Continue towards the second beech hedge.

3. At the second beech hedge, turn right and continue towards the road.

4. Cross the road and follow the footpath straight ahead. Pass through the hedge and continue to the road.

5. At the road, turn right (ignoring the farm track ahead) and follow the road for a short distance. At the sharp right hand bend turn left into the field and follow the footpath along the field edge.

6. Pass through the hedge and follow the footpath across the field, go left as the footpath continues between the two fields towards the farm track.

7. At the track, go left and continue straight ahead towards the road, passing the two cottages.

8. At the road, turn left and walk to the junction, then continue straight ahead between Ebridge Mill and the North Walsham and Dilham Canal. Take care when walking along this road as it can be very busy.

9. Just before the brow of the hill, by the pill box, turn left into the field and follow the footpath along the field edge. Continue following the footpath as it crosses the fields and gently descends towards Meeting Hill. This part of the walk has panoramic views to Honing/Witton (east), White Horse Common/North Walsham (west) and Bacton Wood (north)

10. At the road, turn left and follow the road as it winds through the pretty hamlet of Meeting Hill.

11. At Swan Farm, turn left (signed Briggate) and continue along this lane, passing the tower mill, until you reach the gatehouse.

12. At the gatehouse, turn left and follow Weavers' Way to Honing Station.*

** An alternative route is possible here. Continue along the road into the hamlet of Briggate. At the junction, turn left, and follow the road, walking by the remains of Briggate Mill, then crossing the canal bridge to Honing Station.*

13. Both routes: from the station, cross the road and continue along Weavers' Way. At the farm track (Canal Farm loke, a permissive path) turn left and walk to the road.

14. At the road, turn right and walk to the junction.

15. At the junction, turn right and head towards the village.

16. At the Old Forge, turn left and follow the footpath up the hill to the church. Continue through the churchyard back to your car.

Points of Interest

1. Honing

Honing is a small village with a long history. Evidence of Neolithic settlements have been found in the area. Its name derives from Old English Haninga - 'Han' meaning rock or hill and 'Ingas' meaning people of. It was mentioned in the Domesday Book of 1086.

From approximately 1913 to the early 1980s, the fields surrounding the village would have looked very different from the way they do today. Norfolk is not usually associated with fruit growing, but Honing once had thriving apple and pear orchards. In addition to apples and pears, gooseberries, blackcurrants and redcurrants were also grown. Produce was sent to market in the Midlands and sold from a farm shop in the village.

St Peter's and St Paul's church has also undergone significant change in its long history. Built in the fifteenth century, its most outstanding feature is the tall perpendicular tower with a large west window. In 1795, the church underwent major rebuilding, with the chancel reduced in length and each side aisle reduced in width by about five feet. The nave and aisles were then covered by a single span roof. In 1928-31, the interior of the church was remodelled, the box pews and ceiling were removed and new bench pews, pulpit and communion rail were installed, carved by Cornish and Gaymer of North Walsham from oak grown on the Honing Estate. There are several memorials and ledger stones to members of the Cubitt (who still live in Honing Hall) and Chamber families. There are also two funerary hatchments for Thomas Cubitt (1760-1829) and Edward George Cubitt (1795-1865).

The only memorial brass in the church commemorates Nicholas Parker. Very little is known of his life except a few basic facts. He was born around the 1420s and spent his early life as a soldier in France, later becoming an MP for Dulwich in Suffolk and in 1462 was a Deputy Sheriff of Norwich. The brass, which was made in Norwich, depicts him as a young man in full armour with a lead shield at his feet. He successfully negotiated fifteenth century politics, switching sides from Lancaster to York during the War of the Roses. In the 1460s and 1470s, through marriage and purchase, he acquired land in Honing and other parts of Norfolk. Although a prominent person in the village at the time the church was built, it is not known if he played any part in its construction. Nicholas Parker owned a house in Norwich, but the fact he chose to be buried in Honing suggests his principal residence was in the village. The location of this house is unknown. He died on 19th March 1496 (1497 in the modern calendar). A missal (illuminated service book) belonging to him survives in Cambridge University Library.

Honing was the birthplace of a former archdeacon of York. The son of the village blacksmith, Charles Robert Forder (1907-2008) attended Paston Grammar School in North Walsham and then gained a First in mathematics at Cambridge University. He entered the ministry in the Diocese of York and was archdeacon of York 1957-1972.

2. Ebridge Mill and the North Walsham and Dilham Canal

The North Walsham and Dilham Canal is the name given to the canalisation of the River Ant from Antingham Ponds to Wayford Bridge, a distance of 8¾ miles, with a rise of 58 feet over the course of its length. As the waterway does not follow the river bed it is a true canal, rather than a river navigation and as such is the only locked canal in Norfolk. It was designed as a sailing canal, hence its width and the absence of a tow path. The canal was designed by John Millington of Hammersmith and was his only canal building project. Construction was carried out by Thomas Hughes (who had worked on the Caledonian, Dingwall and Union canals in Scotland) using 100 navies from Bedfordshire, at a cost of £32,000.

The Act of Parliament authorising the construction of the canal was passed in 1811, however, work did not begin until 1825, due to a legal dispute. The River Ant had been navigable up to Dilham before 1810. An Issac Lewis, who worked wherries out of Dilham Staithe, feared the canal would have an adverse effect on his business. In 1825, Mr Lewis was awarded £1,500 compensation by the County Sessions, thus enabling work on the canal to commence. It was formally opened on 29th August 1826.

The canal has five locks, Honing, Ebridge Mill, Briggate Mill, Bacton Wood Mill and Swaffield. The lock size limited the wherries to a length of 50 feet, a beam of 12 feet 4 inches and a draft of 3 feet 6 inches. Cargoes carried included offal to the bone mills at Antingham, fertiliser, manure, flour, grain, farm produce and coal. The transportation of coal never reached the level expected; coal dues were expensive. It remained cheaper to land coal on the beaches of Mundesley or Bacton and transport it overland to North Walsham.

In 1885, the canal was sold to Edward Press of Bacton Wood Mill, who owned a fleet of wherries, for £660. Press died in 1906 and the canal was sold again in 1907. In 1921, it was bought by E.G. Cubitt and G. Walker, millers at Ebridge, for £1,500 and transferred to the North Walsham Canal Company Limited. The canal was damaged in the 1912 flood and the upper reaches from Antingham to Swaffield were abandoned and de-watered in 1927. It continued in use until 1934 when the last wherry, Ella, sailed from Bacton Wood Mill. A section of the canal from Ebridge has been restored.

The five storey mill at Ebridge was built in the early nineteenth century. The mill operated in conjunction with Ebridge tower mill which stood close by. Originally powered by water, an oil engine had been installed by 1937. In 1968, it was converted to electricity and the waterwheel was removed in 1972. Much of the original machinery was removed in 1966 when a new provender mill was built alongside the existing mill building. Between 1869 and 1998 it was owned and operated by Cubitt and Walker Ltd, whose name is still visible on the east side of the building. In 1998, the mill was sold to Duffields, who closed it shortly afterwards, transferring the business to their mill at Saxlingham Thorpe. Following closure, the provender mill was demolished and the old mill and granary building were converted to housing.

3. Meeting Hill

The small hamlet of Meeting Hill is part of the parish of Worstead. During the medieval period the villages around North Walsham and Aylsham were a centre for the weaving of worsted cloth. In the twelfth century, Edward III encouraged Flemish weavers to settle in the area. Worstead prospered and was granted a market in 1336, which continued until the seventeenth century. Originally held on a Tuesday, it changed to Friday to avoid competition with the market at nearby Sutton. The oldest Act of Parliament kept in the House of Lords record office dates from 1497 and concerns apprentices in the worsted industry.

Meeting Hill takes its name from the Baptist meeting house which stands in the centre of the settlement. The chapel was built in 1829, when 120 members of the congregation at (what was then) the Baptist chapel at Smallburgh left to start on their own at Meeting Hill. Meeting Hill had its own branch of the North Walsham and Dilham Canal.

4. Briggate

Briggate is another hamlet of Worstead, although much of the mill site and Old Hall Farm are actually in the parish of Honing. This tiny settlement was once dominated by a large watermill which stood on the road edge. A mill was in existence on this site in 1793, although many of the buildings that were present in the twentieth century dated from the mid-nineteenth century. In its final version, the mill was three storeys high, with a brick base from which rose a timber frame clad in weatherboarding; this was later replaced with grey painted corrugated iron. Originally powered by a fourteen feet diameter, six feet wide, breastshot waterwheel, in 1890 a steam roller mill was installed, eventually replaced by electricity. The waterwheel was removed in 1955. Once employing twelve men, the mill closed in 1969 with its work being transferred to Ebridge.

There were plans to convert the building to residential use, but in August 1975 the site fell victim to an insurance fraud. Purchased for £10,500, the mill was insured for £175,000 and then deliberately burned down. Four men were eventually found guilty of attempting to defraud the insurance company. Due to the difficulty in ascertaining who owned the site, the burnt out shell stood abandoned for many years. Fire damage and weathering made the old granary building unsafe, and in 2012 North Norfolk District Council took the decision to demolish the remains. The local community is hoping to turn the area into a public space, but so far attempts have not been successful.

Briggate tower mill was built around 1850, it had a traditional Norfolk boat shaped cap. Bought by Cubitt and Walker Ltd in 1881, it worked in conjunction with their watermill. By 1949 the mill was derelict, it was eventually converted to residential use. The cap was removed in 2019.

5. Honing Railway Station and the Midland and Great Northern Railway Company

Railways came relatively late to rural North Norfolk and often struggled to make money, particularly in the mid-twentieth century. Honing railway station was part of the Midland and Great Northern Joint Railway (M& GNJR). At 183 miles in length, it was the longest joint railway in Britain. It connected south Lincolnshire with North Norfolk. As its name suggests the M&GNJR was jointly owned by the Midland Railway and the Great Northern Railway; through the parent companies' network it had access to Leicester and the Midlands. Incorporated in 1893, it developed from a number of independent railway concerns which existed in the area. The

M&GNJR survived as an independent company in 1924 when the 'big four' railway companies (London and North Eastern, London Midland and Scottish, Southern and Great Western Railways) were created.

The line which ran through Honing was originally known as the Great Yarmouth Light Railway. In 1878, it was granted permission to extend the line to North Walsham and changed its name to the Yarmouth and North Norfolk Railway (Y&NN), reaching Stalham in 1880 and Honing in August 1882. In 1880, the Y&NN and the Lynn to Fakenham Railway received approval to build a line from North Walsham to Melton Constable, which would connect their two systems. These two companies and two others were amalgamated by the Eastern and Midland Railway Act of 1882, and eventually became part of the M&GNJR.

For such a small rural station, the two platforms, at 400 feet, appear to be very long. However, during the summer months, the station had to accommodate long trains travelling from Leicester and the Midlands with holiday makers destined for Great Yarmouth. In addition to passengers, the railway transported agricultural produce, including livestock. The station closed on 2nd March 1959 and buildings were locked and left. Vegetation growth and weathering caused the waiting rooms to collapse, although the platforms and other structures survive, including cattle pens. One of the two signal boxes also survives; it was removed to the Barton House Railway in Wroxham. Norfolk Railway Heritage Group and Norfolk County Council are working together to expose and preserve the remains of the station.

6. Corner Common Farm

Corner Common Farm House is one of the oldest buildings surviving in Honing. Dating from the early eighteenth century, it is a thatched brick and flint farmhouse with later alterations.

7. River Farm

River Farm barns and buildings have been converted to residential use.

8. Canal Farm

Canal Farm is a two storey, early eighteenth century thatched farmhouse with a patterned brick front and irregularly spaced windows.

3
2
4
1
8
6
7
5
9
8

Walk 2: *Honing, Crostwight and East Ruston*

Summary
This walk uses mainly country lanes and footpaths. For most of the route it is relatively easy walking, there is one flight of steps to access a footpath. The walk is mainly through a landscape of arable fields, heath land and small villages. There are open views to the surrounding countryside.

The Route
Distance: 5¾ miles.
Time: 2½/3 hours.
Suggested car park: St. Peter and St. Paul's Church, Honing, NR28 9QW.
TG 3262 2800
Map Sheet: OS Explorer 0L40

1. From the car park, turn left onto Honing Long Lane. Follow the road for approximately one mile, passing Honing Hall and Hall Farm. Along this road are two mile stones which were buried in about 1939 and not rediscovered until quite recently.

2. At the crossroads turn right, (signed East Ruston). (*At this point it is possible to take a detour to visit the unique church of All Saints', Crostwight)*. Continue along this road as it winds its way past Crostwight Hall and the cottages with the unusual name of The Bleach.

3. The road continues through Crostwight Heath. *It is possible to take a detour here to explore this rare habitat. Take the restricted byway to the left, on reaching the road, cross it going left and follow the footpath (to the right) to rejoin the route.*

4. Ignore the road to the left, and continue towards Fox Hill. Go right at the sharp bend, ignoring the track to the left.

5. At the road junction go straight ahead, signed Fox Hill Road. Follow this road until you reach the crossroads by East Ruston Primary School. From this road there are distant views of Happisburgh church and lighthouse and East Ruston Old Vicarage Gardens (which are open to the public) hidden behind the trees by East Ruston church.

6. At the crossroads, turn right (signed Honing/East Ruston) and continue along this road for approximately one mile, passing The Furze and the Butchers Arms (ignore the roads to the left). Eventually, the road bends sharply to the right at New Bridge over Hundred Stream. Continue to the second sharp right hand bend.

7. At the bend, go left through the hedge and climb the steps up to the field and follow the footpath. Continue following the footpath across the second field, crossing the plank bridge with care. Cross the third field towards the road.

8. At the road, turn right and walk towards the junction. At the junction, turn right and walk towards the T junction. At this junction turn left, signed Briggate/Honing. Continue along this road for a short distance as far as the permissive path (opposite Manor Farmhouse).

9. Turn right onto the permissive path, passing the old barn, and continue to the footpath.

10. Take the footpath to the left and begin the gentle climb back to the car park, taking care when you cross the road.

Points of Interest

1. Honing Hall and Humphrey Repton

Honing Hall is a Grade II* listed building standing at the northern edge of a small park. The present house is the third to stand in this area, it replaced an earlier house which stood close to the present day stable block. That building replaced an even earlier medieval moated dwelling which stood to the north of the present property. The present house was built for B W Chamber, a wealthy worsted weaver from Norwich. The house was completed around 1748; the architect and builder are unknown. Chamber had purchased the estate in the 1740s; his son sold it to Thomas Cubitt in 1784, and his descendents still live in the house. A full height semi-circular extension, designed by Sir John Soane (1753-1837), was added in 1788/90. A new service wing was added to the north, designed by Richard Phipson (1827-1884), in 1868.

In 1792, the landscape designer Humphrey Repton (1752-1818) was commissioned to redesign the existing parkland, for which he produced one of his famous 'before and after' Red Books, which still survives. (These books showed the landowner, by means of flaps and other devices, what the existing landscape looked like and how it would look if the suggested scheme was carried out). Repton also recommended alterations to the exterior of the house to make it more aesthetically pleasing. Repton's suggestions, for the park, included altering the line of the entrance drives, extending the park to the south and creating a rise in the ground there and altering and screening the kitchen garden from view of the house. Many of Repton's recommendations were carried out and the park is regarded as one of the most attractive smaller (74 acres) eighteenth century designed landscapes in Norfolk.

Repton is relatively unknown outside East Anglia, certainly when compared to Lancelot 'Capability' Brown (1716-1783). One reason for this is Repton's clients were country gentry rather than wealthy aristocrats. Whereas Brown expected to carry out his recommended designs, Repton presented his clients with a Red Book, and it was left to them to decide how many, if any, of his recommendations were followed.

2. Crostwight

Once a parish in its own right, Crostwight was merged with its larger neighbour, Honing, in 1935 to form a single civil parish. They became a joint ecclesiasical parish in the late twentieth century. The name Crostwight is a mixture of Old English 'cros' meaning a cross and Old Norse 'thveit' meaning 'meadow or clearing'. So the name means 'a meadow or clearing by a cross'. Mesolithic/Neolithic flint axe heads have been found in the parish and Crostwight was mentioned in the Domesday Book of 1086. It is one of the few places to have a surviving household survey dating back to the Peasants Revolt of 1381. The heads of households were: nine cultivators, three weavers, two spinsters, one dyer and one fuller. The Peasants Revolt was unrest, across England, against the introduction of an unpopular poll tax. In Norfolk, it began on 14th June 1381 and lasted about a fortnight. In the north and east of the county, rebel activity concentrated on burning Manor Court records, including those of the Abbey of St Benet's at Holme. One of the Norfolk rebels came from Crostwight.

The parish church of All Saints' and its Rectory stand some distance away from the present day settlement. The church was built in the thirteenth century and restored in the nineteenth. Externally, the most noticeable feature of the church is the tower stump with its 'hat'. The tower was reduced in height in 1910 after ivy growth had made it unstable. The 'hat' was added to give protection to what remained of the tower. The church has a number of medieval wall paintings and they are one of the most extensive in East Anglia. Those on the north wall date from the late fourteenth or early fifteenth century and have been called the Crostwight Passion Cycle. All the scenes are fragmentary and many are unclear, they include: Christ's entry into Jerusalem, the Last Supper, the Arrest in the Garden of Gethsemane, the Crucifixion, and what may be the Resurrection. Other paintings include the Seven Deadly Sins and two women approaching the gates of heaven, these were discovered in 1840, but again date to the late fourteenth century. The rood screen remains, but has been restored and is not painted.

The Rectory is now a private house.

3. Crostwight Heath

Crostwight Heath, a County Wildlife Site, is a mixture of heathland, woodland and gorse scrub. It supports a range of flora and fauna including heath bedstraw, roe deer and small copper butterflies. During World War II it was used as a training area.

4. Crostwight Hall

Crostwight Hall was built in the mid-sixteenth century, re-using medieval ecclesiastical stone. In 1720, the hall was acquired by Robert Walpole, but by the end of the eighteenth century the main buildings were in ruin. As a consequence, the service buildings were converted into a new hall. In the late twentieth century the old hall and its outbuildings, including the new hall, a large barn and a brewhouse were restored and converted into residential properties.

5. East Ruston

East Ruston has a long history. Its name is Old English and means a brushwood enclosure. The earliest datable archaeological finds in the village are Neolithic. St Mary's church, which stands about one mile to the east of the main settlement area, was built mainly in the fourteenth century; it was altered in the fifteenth, eighteenth and nineteenth centuries. The tower once had a spire, which is unusual for Norfolk. The rood screen remains. In 1980, the church was made redundant and is now under the care of the Redundant Churches Trust.

East Ruston was the birthplace of the Classical scholar, Richard Porson (1759-1808), eldest son of Higgin Porson, the Parish Clerk. Educated in village schools, he entered Trinity College, Cambridge in 1778, and received his BA in 1782 and MA in 1785. Elected a Fellow of Trinity College in 1782, he lost the fellowship a decade later when he decided not to take Holy Orders and was not nominated for one of the two lay fellowships. As Porson had no means of support, his friends got up a subscription to provide an annuity. Porson agreed to accept the interest during his lifetime, the principle was to be returned to the donors on his death. When he died, this sum was used to fund the Porson prize (awarded for Greek verse composition) in 1816 and the Porson Scholarship, first awarded in 1855. In 1792, he was elected Regius Professor of Greek, which he remained until his death in 1808, and in 1806 he was appointed principal librarian of the newly formed London Institution.

To the east of the primary school, is the village hall, gifted to the village in 1925 by Sir James Roll (1846-1927), Chairman of Pearl Assurance Company and Lord Mayor of London 1920-21. Roll was born in East Ruston where his father was a tenant farmer. He left the village school at the age of about twelve to work on a local farm, later travelling, by sea, from Great Yarmouth to London. In London, he began his career as an office boy to an agent of Pearl Assurance, becoming Chairman in 1892, and retiring in 1916. In that year, Roll became Master of the Glovers Livery Company.

East Ruston's literary claim to fame comes from its appearance in a Sherlock Holmes story 'The Adventure of the Dancing Men' by Arthur Conan-Doyle (1859-1930), as the location of Abe Slaney's hideaway (Elridge's Farm).

6. East Ruston Poor's Allotment

Medieval farming was based on an open field system, with large fields divided into strips, which were then allotted to yeomen and tenant farmers. As a result an individual's 'farm' could be spread across the open field. This system required the holders of adjoining strips to plant the same crops and was increasingly seen as a barrier to innovation and improvement. Enclosure, the process of combining strips into a single field owned or rented by an individual, began as early as the twelfth century. From the sixteenth century consolidation of strips was seen as the most economical way of farming. Enclosure of land was usually by informal agreement, however, from the seventeenth century authorisation by Act of Parliament became increasingly common; from the mid-eighteenth century it became the norm. The initiative to enclose could come from landowners seeking to maximise the rental value of their land or farmers wishing to improve their farms. One of the consequences of enclosure was the loss of access, for the rural poor, to common land and woodland for grazing and gathering fuel. In some cases, those with certain legal or manorial rights were granted an allotment of land in compensation. In Norfolk, of the 420 Enclosure Acts between 1720 and 1834, 234 (56%) made special provision for poor inhabitants. Compensation was made not by individual allotment of land but by collective allotment vested in a parish authority. East Ruston is such a case.

The East Ruston Enclosure Act of 1806 and the Enclosure Award of 1810 enclosed 771 acres of common and waste ground. Of those, 300 acres were awarded to the trustees of the poor in the form of a poor's allotment. The 1806 Act specified the uses to which the land could be put and who could benefit from it. The poor were defined as anyone who did not occupy tenements of more than five pounds per annum or more than ten acres of land. The land could be used for cutting peat, and as common pasture for grazing cattle, sheep and geese. In the 1870s, some of the land was sold to the Eastern and Midland Railway for the construction of their line from Great Yarmouth to North Walsham. The trustees still administer the land getting income from shooting rights, fishing lakes and the Rural Payment Agency and continue to distribute funds within the village.

7. East Ruston Old Vicarage Gardens

The Old Vicarage Gardens have been described as one of the most important gardens created in Norfolk in the twentieth century. Its location close to the sea gives it a milder, maritime climate, which allows a range of plants, some tender and rare, to be grown. The gardens around the house (which was built in 1913 in the Arts and Craft style) were begun in the 1970s and then extended so that they now cover 13 hectares (32 acres). The gardens are open to the public on certain days.

8. Honing and East Ruston Commons

This area was once the site of a large lake known as Honing Broad. Further to the north, (shown on an estate map of land belonging to Robert Walpole) was a smaller body of water known as Crostwight Water.

9. Bush Farmhouse

This brick and flint farmhouse dates to the sixteenth century and is one of the oldest surviving houses in Honing.

Also see Points of Interest for Walk 1.

Notes about walk

2
7
3
1
4
5
6

Walk 3: *Around Blakeney*

Summary

This walk uses footpaths, tracks and country lanes. It is generally level, although there is a steep climb up from the coastal path to Blakeney Downs. The route passes through Blakeney, then follows the coast path towards Morston, where there are views across the salt marshes, before heading inland. There are panoramic views of Blakeney Point and Blakeney outer harbour from Blakeney Downs. The walk heads back to Blakeney village through arable fields. It is possible to take a short detour to explore the heathland landscape of Wiveton Downs.

The Route

Distance: 4½ miles.
Time: 2/2½ hours.
Suggested car park: Blakeney Village Hall, Langham Road, Blakeney, NR25 7PG.
TG 0254 4380
Map Sheet: OS Explorer 251
Alternative car parking: Wiveton Downs car park or Blakeney Quay

1. Leave the car park and cross the A149 with care and walk down Westgate Street, passing the Kings Arm's, whose roof informs you it dates from 1760.

2. At the Quay, go left, passing the village sign, and follow the coast path towards Morston.

3. Ignore the footpath to the left and continue along the sea bank for approximately ¾ of a mile. Just before the wooden steps, turn left and take the bridleway which climbs up from the marsh to the road, passing 'North Down'.

4. Before crossing the road take a moment to look back and enjoy the views of Blakeney Point and outer harbour. Cross the road with care and take the footpath to the right, follow it around the old quarry. This path affords good views of Morston church.

5. The path follows the field in a generally southerly direction, before heading east towards the woodland. Follow the path around the edge of the woodland. There are distant views of the poultry houses on Langham Airfield and Langham church.

6. At the driveway, turn right, following the footpath to reach the road. Here there are views of Blakeney Point and Blakeney village.

7. Cross the road and follow the bridleway towards New Barn Farm. Follow the footpath through the farmyard and continue until the path meets the road.

At this point it is possible to make a detour to explore Wiveton Downs Site of Special Scientific Interest (SSSI). Cross the road and follow the path along the edge of the Downs. You can take one of the paths which lead off this path onto the heathland; or continue to the road, turn left, then after a short distance, climb the steps up to Wiveton Downs car park, from where you can explore this part of the site. Make the reverse journey to return to the route.

8. Turn left (right if you are returning from the detour) and follow the road towards Blakeney. Along this road are views towards Cley and Wiveton.

9. On entering Blakeney village, take the footpath to the left (The Butts). At the end of the footpath turn right and follow the road back to the car park.

Points of Interest

1. Blakeney

The name Blakeney is Old English meaning 'an island or dry ground in a marsh'. Finds from the Mesolithic, Neolithic and Bronze ages have been found in the area but no distinct settlement has been found. Blakeney does not appear in the Domesday Book of 1086; however, a settlement called Sniterley (meaning a clearing belonging to Snytra) was included. It is not clear whether Blakeney and Sniterley were separate settlements, or if Sniterley gradually became known as Blakeney. Sniterley was not a large settlement but it did have a church.

One of the oldest buildings to survive in Blakeney is St Nicholas' church, which dates mainly to the fourteenth and fifteenth century. The chancel is thirteenth century in date and the nave and tower date to 1435. The church has examples of sixteenth century graffiti, in the form of sailing ships.

During the medieval period Blakeney was a thriving port, documentary evidence shows it was well established by 1250. Blakeney was one of the Glaven ports which grew up around the mouth of the River Glaven. Trade in salt fish was important, and the Glaven ports were known to have supplied cod and ling to London. Blakeney also traded with countries as far away as Iceland. In 1301, Blakeney sent two ships to Berwick to help in Edward I's war effort. The one reminder of this prosperity visible today is the Guildhill, the brick vaulted undercroft of a wealthy merchant's house dating to the fourteenth or fifteenth century. Next to the Guildhall is Mariners Hill, an artificial mound of unknown date and use, which could have been a beacon mount.

During the post medieval period a number of earth banks were constructed on the marshes in an attempt by local landowners to reclaim land which was becoming salt marsh. These reclamation schemes encouraged the silting up of the estuary and the decline of the Glaven ports. A decline which was further hastened by the arrival of larger steam ships and the railways in the nineteenth century, which made transport cheaper and faster.

2. Blakeney Point

Blakeney Point is a four mile long spit of shingle and sand dunes which together with the salt marshes on its landwards side form Blakeney National Nature Reserve. During the nineteenth century the area was used for wildfowling. In 1912 a public appeal enabled the land to be purchased from the Calthorpe Estate. It was donated to the National Trust. University

College, London established a research centre in the Old Lifeboat station which stands towards the end of the spit. The reserve is an important site for nesting birds, especially terns, and a major site for migrating birds. The end of the spit has a colony of approximately 500 harbour and common seals. The spit is gradually moving westwards and landwards. Between 1886 and 1925 it lengthened by 132.1 metres (433 feet). As it moved landwards, it obstructed the Glaven channel, leading to flooding in Cley. In 2007 the Environment Agency decided to create a new route for the river south of its original line, at a cost of £1.5 million.

One of the most prominent structures on Blakeney Point is the Watch House (also known as Halfway House) which stands 1.5 miles from Cley beach car park. It was built in 1835, by HM Customs and Excise as a lookout for smugglers, more recently it has been used by the Girl Guides (until the 1990s) and as a holiday let.

3. Blakeney Downs

Blakeney Downs forms part of the Blakeney Esker, a ridge of land, 3.5 kilometres in length and between 40-100 metres wide, which runs towards Wiveton. It rises, in places, to 20 metres above the surrounding land. It was formed at a time when much of Norfolk was covered by an ice sheet. Esker is an Irish word meaning 'sandy ridge'. They were formed by rivers flowing under the glacier. As the waterflow slowed deposits of sediment were laid down, as the glacier retreated the sand and gravel remained. The sand and gravel of the esker are very different from the clay of the surrounding countryside; producing a heathland and acid grassland habitat which supports common heather, bell heather, common gorse, bracken and bedstraw.

4. Wiveton Downs

Wiveton Downs forms the southern end of the Blakeney Esker and is now an SSSI. It is also an area of open access with numerous paths by which visitors can explore this unique landscape. From the 1940s until the 1980s, the area was quarried for sand and gravel. Much of the material went into the construction of local World War II airfields, such as nearby Langham. By the 1980s most of the usable gravel had been removed. Quarrying exposed the structure of the esker and allowed scientists to understand how it was formed. The esker formed in association with the Cromer Ridge, which runs from Overstrand to Holt.

5. St Andrew's and St Mary's Church, Langham

St Andrew's and St Mary's church Langham dates mainly from the fourteenth century. Its thirteenth century font has an interesting example of graffiti. The north window was designed by Sir Edward Burne-Jones (1833-1898) for Morris & Co in 1894. Buried in the churchyard is Captain Frederick Marryat (1792-1848), who lived in Manor Cottage, author of the classic children's novel 'The Children of the New Forest' (1847).

6. Langham Airfield

Langham Airfield operated between 1941 and 1960. On the eastern edge of the airfield is Langham Dome, built in 1942, it was a state of the art training facility for anti-aircraft gunners. At twenty-five feet high and with a diameter of 40 feet, it is one of only six such domes in existence and is now a scheduled ancient monument. The Dome is open to the public on certain days of the year. After closure, the airfield was purchased by Bernard Matthews Ltd and poultry houses were constructed on the former concrete runways.

7. All Saints Church, Morston

The tower and nave are twelfth or thirteenth century in date, the nave, aisles and chancel early fourteenth century. The porches were added in the fifteenth and sixteenth centuries. The tower was damaged by a lightning strike in 1743 and the church underwent restoration in the nineteenth century. The church has the base of a painted rood screen of 1480.

Notes about walk

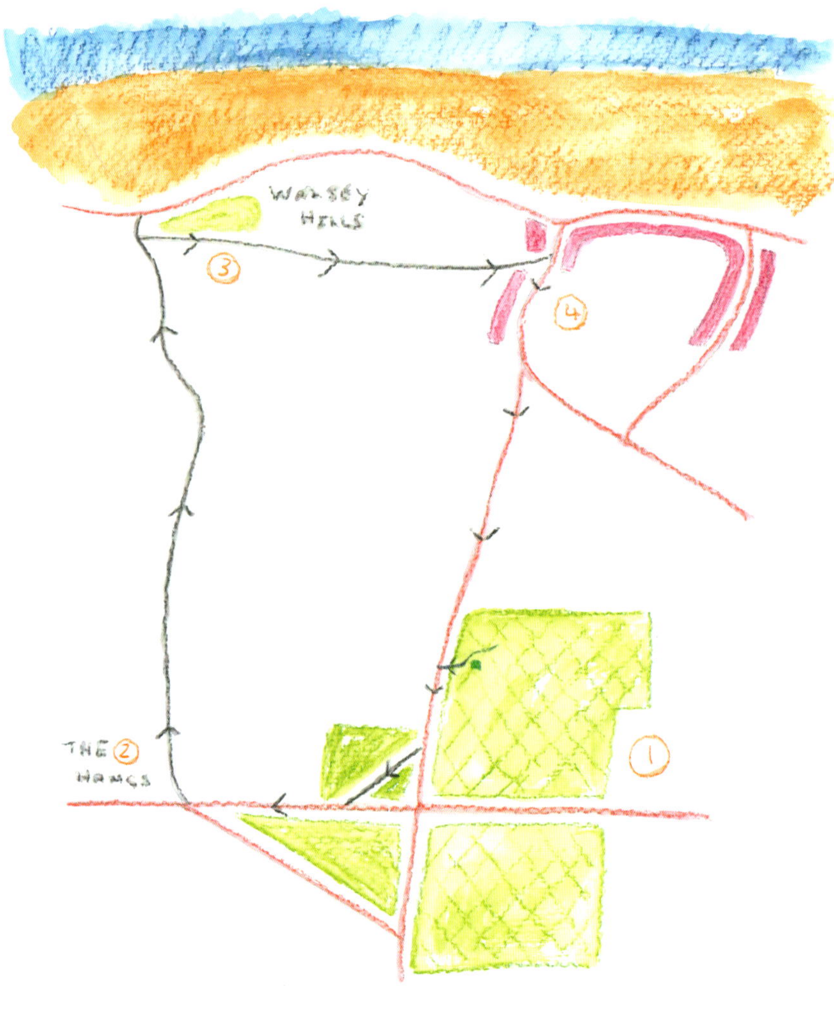
HILLS
3
4
THE 2
1

Walk 4: *Around Salthouse*

Summary

This walk uses country lanes and footpaths, it is generally easy, but there are some uneven surfaces. There is a steep climb from Salthouse village to Salthouse Heath. The walk starts in a heathland setting and then passes through arable fields, with view of the salt marshes and sea, descending into the village of Salthouse, before returning to heathland once more.

The Route

Distance: 3 miles.
Time: 1½/2 hours.
Suggested car park: Salhouse Heath. (NR25 7AJ gives Salthouse Village Store, Coast road) TG 0720 4290
Map Sheet: OS Explorer 251
Alternative car parking: Limited roadside parking at Cley Hangs

1. From the car park, turn left and follow the track to the road.

2. At the road, turn left and follow the road for approximately ¼ of a mile, then turn right, taking the footpath across the heathland.

3. At the road, turn right and continue to Cley Hangs.

4. At Cley Hangs (just before the road junction), turn right and follow the footpath as it descends towards Walsey Hills.

5. At Walsey Hills, ignoring the path to the left, go right and head across the field following the footpath, heading towards Salthouse.

6. Go through the kissing gate and continue following the footpath, which becomes narrow as it passes between the gardens.

7. At the road, turn right and head back to Salthouse Heath and the car park.

Points of Interest

1. Salthouse Heath and the Baggot Goats

Salthouse Heath, and its neighbour Kelling Heath, is an example of a glacial outwash plain. Lying at the edge of the Cromer Ridge, the heath was formed by meltwater running from the glacier in braided channels depositing sediments in a fan shape. This coastal heathland covers an area of 99 hectares, with rare acid dry heath on the northern section (which is home to the rarest plant on the heath - the May Lily), while the southern section is mainly oak and birch woodland. The gorse on the coastal slope attracts a wide range of wildlife, including buzzards, red kite, linnet, adders and common lizards.

Salthouse Heath was an area of great activity during the Bronze Age, with many burial mounds dotted over the site, these included a cluster of thirty which represent possibly the largest Bronze Age cemetery in Norfolk. There are at least nine large barrow mounds and a large number of smaller ones. The mounds have survived partly because the area is unsuitable for agriculture. During the medieval period it was used for grazing sheep, while gorse was cut to make 'faggots' which were used as the base of haystacks.

There are the remains of a World War II radar station on the heath, which operated 1942-circa 1960.

As part of a management scheme for the heathland, baggot goats have recently been introduced. Baggot goats were introduced into England in the 1380s, probably returning with the Crusaders. It is thought they have a common ancestry with goats in the Rhone valley. Richard II is said to have given the goats to John Baggot of Blithfield Hall, Staffordshire and they have lived there, semi-wild, ever since.

The goats have no commercial value, but are used for conservation grazing. The Baggot goats of Norfolk winter on Salthouse Heath, while spending the summer months grazing the cliff slopes at Cromer.

2. Cley Hangs

To the right of the footpath is a bowl barrow, a scheduled ancient monument, which is thought to be related to the barrows on Salthouse Heath. In 1924, there was limited excavation of the site. Bowl barrows are funerary mounds which date from the late Neolithic to the late Bronze Age.

The site consists of an earth mound encircled by a ditch c1.5 metres high and c15 metres in diameter. The earth from the ditch was used to create the mound. The ditch has been partly infilled.

3. Walsey Hills

Walsey Hills is a 1.2 hectares (3 acres) reserve on the edge of the A149 between Cley and Salthouse. It is owned by the Norfolk Ornithologists Association and is open from dawn to dusk. It has far reaching views across the coastal marshes and the Cley Marshes Norfolk Wildlife Trust reserve. Steps from the footpath lead up to the site. Between 1958 and 1968, it was the site of a Royal Observer Corp underground monitoring post and fallout shelter in the event of a nuclear war.

4. Salthouse

The name Salthouse comes from Old English and Old Norse for 'house for storing salt'. The area has had a very long history of human settlement. The earliest datable find is a Paleaolithic flint flake, although there is some doubt about the object's authenticity. There was a possible Roman signal station on Grainborough Hill. The settlement was well established by the time of the Domesday survey of 1086. On the coast road is a section of seventeenth century flint wall which could be part of a former quay wall.

St Nicholas' church is the oldest surviving building in the village. Of late Perpendicular style, it was rebuilt in the fifteenth century by Sir Henry Heydon. The church has the remains of a repainted rood screen and examples of ship graffiti.

Notes about walk

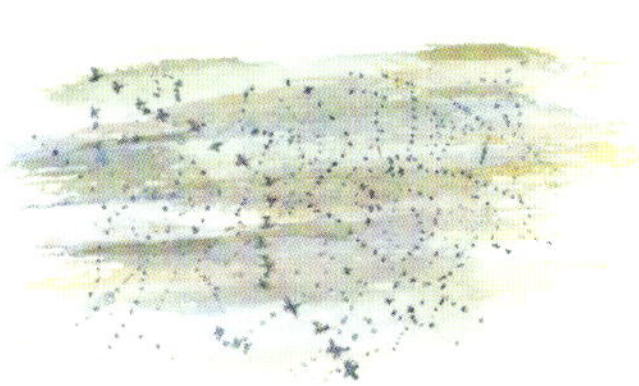

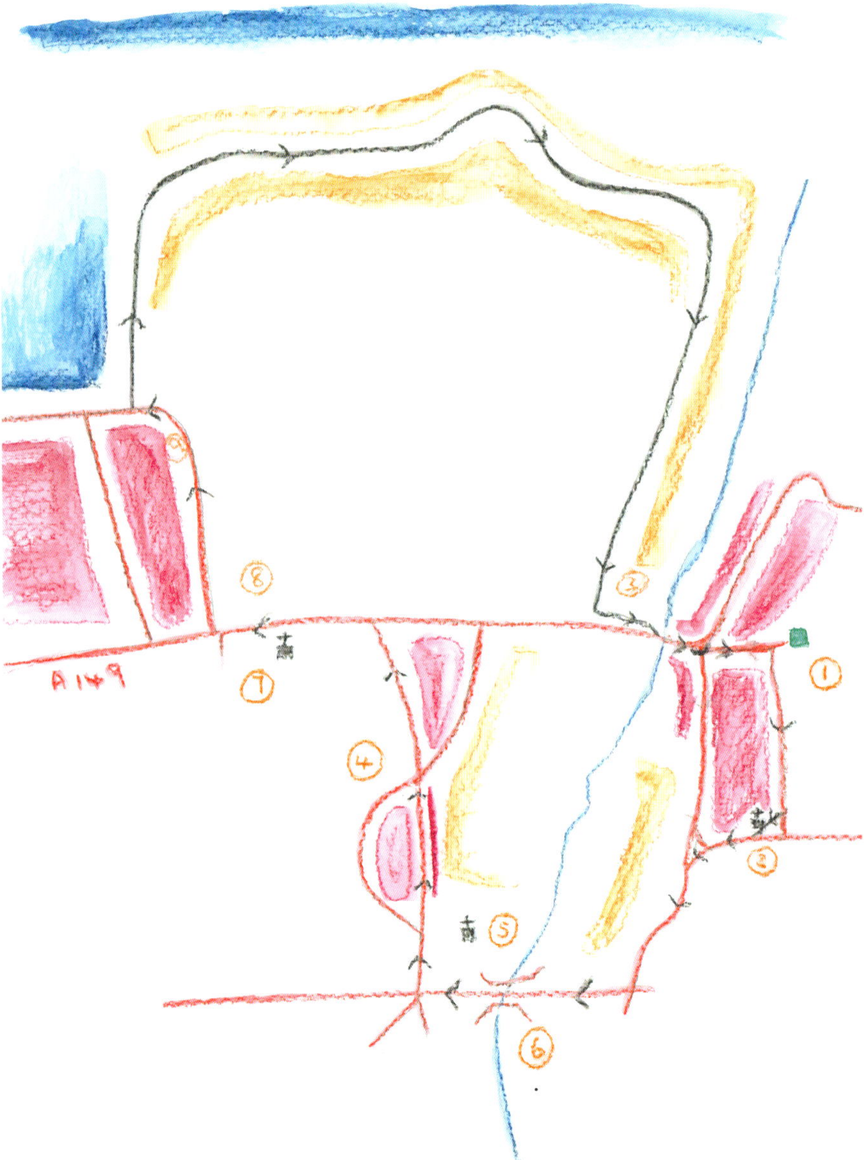

A149
1
2
3
4
5
6
7
8
9

Walk 5: *Cley, Wiveton and Blakeney*

Summary

This walk uses country lanes and the Norfolk coast path, which follows sea defence banks. The scenery on the walk changes from arable fields and meadows to salt and freshwater marshes. It starts in the village of Cley and heads towards Wiveton, crossing the River Glaven by a narrow medieval bridge. From Wiveton it follows the main coast road to Blakeney, then heads back to Cley via the marshes, where a variety of wildlife is visible.

The Route

Distance: 6 miles.
Time: 2½/3 hours.
Suggested car park: Cley Village Hall, The Fairstead, NR25 7RJ.
TG 0473 4372
Map Sheet: OS Explorer 251
Alternative car parking: Wiveton Village car park

1. From the car park, turn left and follow the road (Church Lane) to the church.

2. Enter the churchyard and follow the footpath to the gate, go through the gate to the road.

3. Cross the road and the green and then go left on to Glandford Road. Continue along this road to the junction. There is a good view of Wiveton church from this road.

4. At the junction, turn right and follow the road (Bridgefoot Lane) over the bridge and the River Glaven, into Wiveton.

5. At the junction turn right and follow the road into Wiveton village. Ignore the road to the left and continue to the second junction.

6. At the junction, go left and continue to the A149.

7. At the junction, go left onto the footpath, then taking care, cross the road and continue (left) along the pavement towards Blakeney.

8. At the crossroads (by the Roman Catholic church), turn right and follow the road as it descends towards the marshes. The road winds past the Manor Hotel and the duck pond.

9. At the Quay car park, turn right and climb onto the sea defence bank and the Norfolk Coast Path. Follow the path as it arches back towards Cley. There are fine views of Blakeney Point and the Watch House (see point of interest 2 of Walk 3), Cley Mill and the marshes.

10. As the path reaches Cley, climb onto the bank and follow the path as it turns left, crossing the River Glaven for a second time, towards the village. Drop down from the bank to road level.

11. Cross the road with care and turn right into Holt Road.

12. After a short distance, turn left into Town Yard and then go right into The Fairstead and head back to the car park.

Points of Interest

1. Cley next the Sea

This is a long established settlement. Cley is Old English meaning 'the place of clayey soil'. The earliest archaeological finds in the village date from the Paleolithic period. Cley appears in the Domesday Book of 1086 as 'Claice'. In the medieval period, Cley developed as an important port, and was one of the busiest ports in England. The village was on the edge of the Glaven River Estuary; the marshes were submerged at high tide allowing boats to navigate up to a harbour situated between Cley and Wiveton churches. Cley was the main port for Holt and the surrounding area. Imports included salt, spices and timber, exports included salt fish, cloth, and grain. Its trading connection with the Low Countries is reflected in the number of Flemish gables to be found in the village. It was also a haven for smugglers and pirates. From the fourteenth to the sixteenth centuries, the Glaven ports (Blakeney, Cley and Wiveton) were one of only three places in Norfolk to have a customs house; the other two being Yarmouth and Lynn. A survey of shipping in 1580 showed the Glaven ports to have 36 ships, compared to 32 in Lynn. In 1253, Cley was granted a weekly market, this was reconfirmed in 1310. From the seventeenth to nineteenth centuries the saltmarshes to the north of the village were drained and reclaimed by the construction of a large sea defence bank. In 1637, a local landowner, Sir Henry Calthorpe, constructed a dam across the river, enclosing the marshes, this action had far reaching consequences. The family were inspired by the success of Cornellius Vermuyden in draining the fens. After two petitions to the King, the bank was demolished in 1649, but the river course had already begun to silt up.

Despite the removal of the bank, siltation continued gradually limiting the size of ships able to access the harbour and international trade began to decline; in 1853 the Customs House was closed. Although still busy in the late nineteenth, the reducing depth of the river, the construction of a new road and the arrival of the railway in Holt (1884), meant the end for Cley as a port. The river was reduced to a narrow reed choked channel. In recent years, the harbour has undergone some restoration and can now take boats up to thirty feet in length. In 1612, Cley suffered a devastating fire during which 117 buildings were destroyed. As a consequence, most of the surviving buildings are post seventeenth century.

Notable people associated with the village include the poet Rupert Brooke who was staying in Cley at the outbreak of World War I and the singer, James Blunt whose family once owned the mill.

2. St Margaret's Church, Cley

The oldest surviving building in Cley is St Margaret's church, the largest and grandest of the churches of the Glaven Ports. The present church was begun in 1320, replacing an earlier building. The rebuilding was largely the responsibility of the merchant de Vaux family. Built in the Early English or Decorated style it was largely complete by the mid 1340s. During the fifteenth century further alterations were made, reflecting the wealth and confidence of the port, including the Perpendicular style south porch. A map of 1586 shows the church with a spire. The transepts and north porch of the church are now ruins. The church has a seven sacraments font, bench ends carved in the form of people and mythical creatures, a Jacobean font of 1611 and bosses. On the south side of the tower is a board which once depicted the Royal Arms of Charles II, overpainted with those of Queen Anne. The practice of displaying Royal Arms dates from the Reformation, it was made compulsory at the restoration of Charles II.

3. Cley Mill

Cley Mill dates to the late eighteenth or early nineteenth centuries; it was not marked on Faden's map of Norfolk of 1797, but was advertised for sale in 1819, when it was described as 'newly erected'. It is five storeys high with a stage at the second floor level and dome shaped cap. Between 1875 and 1921 it was owned by just two families, Farthings and Burroughes. Around 1912, the then owner transferred the business to their windmill at Holt. In 1921, the mill was sold for £350 and converted into a holiday home. The machinery was removed during the conversion. On 1st January 1953 the mill was flooded to a depth of 2.44 metres (8 feet). In 1983, permission was granted to turn the mill into a guesthouse and self-catering units.

4. Wiveton

Like many of the settlements in Norfolk, Wiveton has a long history, with archaeological finds dating back to the Mesolithic period. The name Wiveton is Old English meaning 'Wifa's enclosure', it was mentioned in the Domesday Book of 1086. Wiveton Hall was built in 1652 by John Gifford and was extended in 1908.

For a number of years Wiveton was the home (Double House) to Elizabeth Forster (1908-1995), an ornithologist and knitwear designer. She started working for the BBC in 1930, and from 1945 had a parallel career as a freelance designer of knitting patterns for a number of well known women's magazines, including 'Womens Weekly' and pattern companies such as Wendy. Taking early retirement from the BBC in 1955, Elizabeth Forster moved to North Norfolk, where she combined her enthusiasm for bird watching and knitting, and was known to her fellow bird watchers as 'The Grey Pullover'. She spent the summer months in Norfolk working on her knitting design business, work which financed her travels in search of birds. During the winter months, she travelled (mostly alone) across India, Nepal, Afghanistan, Cambodia, Costa Rica, Mexico, Chile, Peru, Argentina, the Falklands and Australia, using local transport and guides. At the age of 70, she trekked to the Everest base camp. She wrote 'The Wandering Tattler' (a species of bird) about her journeys in South America and Asia. The birds and animals she saw during these trips inspired some of her designs. After Elizabeth Forster's death, in 1995, at the age of 87 years, her collection and archive was acquired by the Norwich Castle Museum.

5. St Mary's Church, Wiveton

St Mary's church dates from the fourteenth (tower and chancel) and mid to late fifteenth centuries (nave aisles and porch), and is Perpendicular in style. It was restored at various times from the seventeenth to nineteenth centuries. The remains of the rood screen were reworked to form a tower screen. It faces its neighbouring church at Cley across what would once have been a tidal estuary. Just east of the churchyard along the river bank would have been Wiveton Quay. The church has a memorial to Frederick Marshman Bailey (1882-1967) a British intelligence officer who was involved in the 'Great Game' (the fight for supremacy between the British and Russians in the Himalayas). His work allowed him to pursue his hobbies of photography, butterfly collecting and trophy hunting in the Tibetan region. He was awarded the Royal Geographical Society's Gold Explorer's medal. Some of his specimens were presented to the Natural History Museum.

6. Wiveton Bridge

Wiveton bridge was built about 1500, of stone and brick. The bridge originally had two arches, the western one being removed, sometime after 1586, as the flow in the river reduced. From the bridge it is possible to see eel, moorhen or even a trout. It was one of two medieval bridges crossing the Glaven at Wiveton. The location of the second bridge is uncertain.

7. St Nicholas' Church, Blakeney

St Nicholas' church, Blakeney was founded in the thirteenth century, but the greater part of the building dates from the fifteenth century. It is unusual in having two towers, a western one at 104 feet tall and shorter eastern one. The eastern tower may possibly have been built to house a single bell, which would be rung to announce the consecration of the elements. Another theory is that it was an aid to navigation for ships entering Blakeney Harbour. The nave of the church has a hammerbeam roof. The chancel has a seven light lancet window. Fragments of medieval stained glass, which survived the Reformation, were incorporated into a window in the north aisle. The church has examples of ship graffiti which date from the sixteenth century. Buried in the churchyard is Sir Henry 'Tim' Birkin (1896-1933), a leading British racing driver of the 1920s, one of the 'Bentley Boys'.

8. Friary Farmhouse

Friary Farmhouse stands on the site of a Carmelite Friary founded around 1296, and dissolved in 1538. Some of the masonry from the friary was used in the construction of Friary Farmhouse. A section of medieval wall, with a gatehouse, survives to the north of the farmhouse.

9. Blakeney Manor Hotel

Blakeney Manor Hotel is a seventeenth century building which has been altered over the years.

10. Blakeney Hotel

Blakeney Hotel on the Quay was built circa 1920 on the site of the former Crown and Anchor public house (reputedly the haunt of smugglers) and opened in 1923.

Also see Points of Interest for Walk 3.

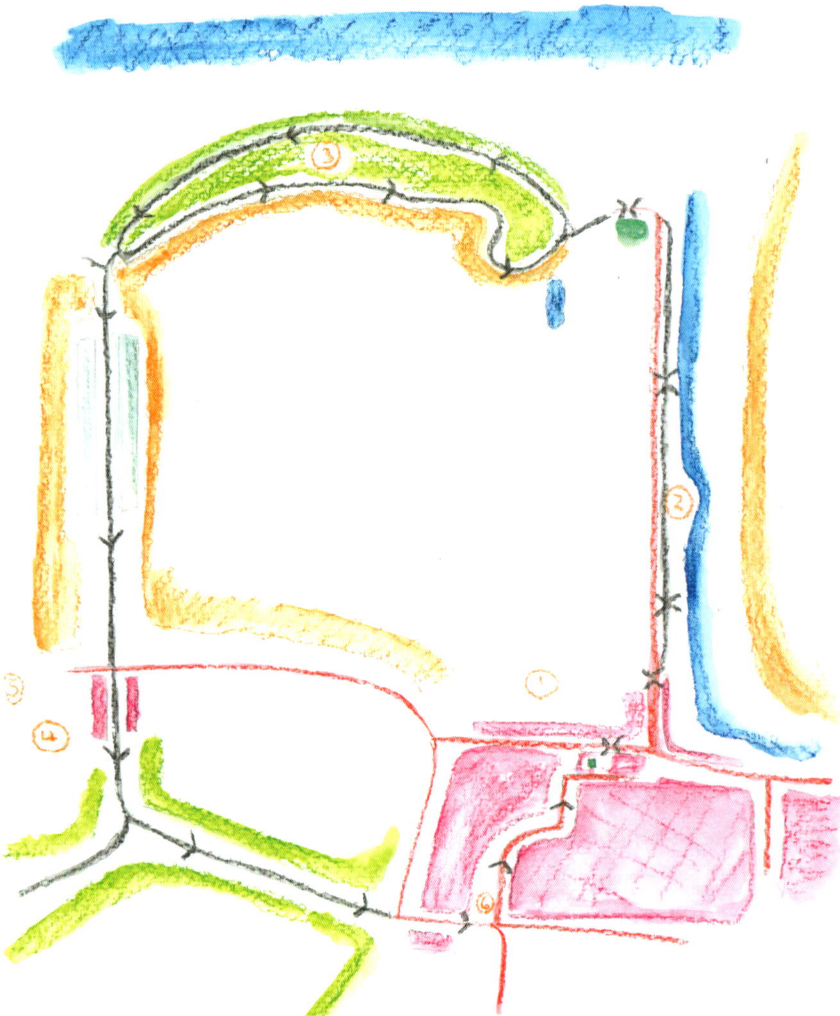
3
2
1
5
4
6

Walk 6: *Wells to Holkham*

Summary

This walk uses footpaths, tracks and country roads, it is generally easy walking, although there is uneven ground in the dunes. The walk leaves the town of Wells-next-the-Sea and heads along the sea defence bank to Wells beach. The bank affords views over the harbour and marshes towards Stiffkey. It then heads into Holkham Nature Reserve and follows the curve of the dunes to Holkham Gap. There are glimpses of the sea through the pines. From the dunes it heads up Lady Anne's Drive, through Holkham village and into the northern part of Holkham Park, where it turns eastwards back towards Wells.

The Route

Distance: 7 miles.
Time: 3/3½ hours.
Suggested car park: North Norfolk District Council Stearmans Yard Car Park, Freeman Street, Wells. NR23 lBA
TF 9145 4383
Map Sheet: OS Explorer 251
Alternative car parking: Beach Road, Wells or Lady Anne's Drive, Holkham

1. Leave the car park via the Freeman Street exit and turn right along Freeman Street and walk towards the Quay.

2. At the mini roundabout, turn left into Beach Road. Go right and walk up onto the sea defence bank.

3. At the end of the bank, turn left and descend to the car park. Cross the car park and head towards the nature reserve.

4. On entering the dunes take the path to the right, signed 'Beach Access'. Ignore paths to the right which give access to the beach and continue along the edge of the dunes. There is no correct path on this part of the walk. Keeping the sea on your right (to the north), follow the gentle curve of the dunes until you reach Holkham Gap.

5. On reaching the Gap, follow the boardwalk away from the sea towards the Lookout cafe.

Here it is possible to take an alternative route back to Wells. Turn left and follow the Norfolk Coast Path back to Wells Beach car park and return to Wells town centre via the sea defence bank. At the mini roundabout, turn right on to Freeman Street and head back to the car park.

For a longer walk:

6. From the Lookout cafe, head through the car park on Lady Anne's Drive and walk towards the road.

7. Cross the road with care and walk through Holkham village into Holkham Park.

8. Once in the park, follow the roadway until it forks, just before the park's main car park. Take the road to the left and head towards the gate.

9. Go through the gate and take the road to the left. Follow this road out of the park and continue along the track to Mill Road.

10. At Mill Road, go right and head back towards Wells, walking by Wells Hospital.

11. At the junction, turn left, then immediately left again into Park Road, then turn right into Theatre Road. Follow this road for a short distance before turning left into Stearman's Yard car park.

Points of Interest

1. Wells-Next-The-Sea

Wells is a small, but very popular, seaside resort and port with a long history of settlement. The earliest archaeological finds date from the Palaeolithic period. It is mentioned in the Domesday Book of 1086 as 'Guella' from 'wella' or the wells - springs which rise from the chalk in the area. In the fourteenth century, 'Juxta Mare' (next the sea) was added to its name to distinguish it from other places of the same name. The hyphens do not appear to have been used until the opening of the Wells and Fakenham Railway in 1857 and were adopted by Wells Urban District Council in 1956.

The prosperity of the town in earlier centuries is evident in the number of buildings which are of historical or architectural interest, for example, The Buttlands, a spacious green surrounded by Georgian houses and Blenheim House on Theatre Road. At one point, Wells had about forty public houses, although most have now been converted to residential use.

Wells has been a seaport since at least the fourteenth century, exporting grain to London and the North East and importing coal. In 1331, there were thirteen fishing boats catching herring and cod. A survey of shipping in 1580 revealed there were nineteen boats of over sixteen tons operating out of port. An Act of Parliament of 1663 set up the Wells Harbour Commissioners to preserve the use of the quay, creeks, channels and landing places of the port of Wells. Today, the commissioners employ a harbourmaster and uniformed officers to patrol the harbour and prevent infringements of the by-laws. The old Customs House on East Quay was mentioned by Samuel Pepys in his diary in 1666. As recently as 1986, Wells port was handling 200 large ships and cargo of 100,000 tons, mostly animal feed.

Malt was another major industry in the town, at its height there were twelve maltings in operation. In 1750, malt accounted for $^1/_3$ of the total exports, mainly to the Netherlands, more than any other port except Great Yarmouth. Some of the maltings buildings survive, one is used as an arts and cultural centre, another (Pauls Maltings) has been converted to residential use. On the Quay is another distinctive building, the granary, built in 1904-5. The high gantry above the road allowed grain to be transferred between the building and ships at the quayside without disrupting traffic. It ceased operating in the 1990s and has been converted for residential use.

The oldest building in the town ought to be the church of St Nicholas, except it is not. Originally constructed about 1200, it was rebuilt in the mid-fifteenth century. This building was destroyed by fire in 1879, so the church you see today is not medieval, but a Victorian reconstruction. Buried in the churchyard is John Fryer (1753-1817), sailing master of HMS Bounty at the time of the mutiny, who was born in the town. At Lieutenant Blyth's Court Martial, Fryer was critical of the actions of both Blyth and Fletcher Christian, although he remained loyal to Blyth. He retired from the Royal Navy in 1812 and returned to Wells, where he died in 1817.

One house now standing in Wells did not begin life in the town. Ware House, off Plummer's Hill, was originally constructed in 1450 in Ware, Hertfordshire. In 1969, its owner, May Savidge (a retired technical illustrator), was informed by her local council that the house was to be demolished to make way for a new roundabout. Undaunted, in 1970 Miss Savidge, then aged 58 years, divided her house into 1000 numbered sections and moved it to Wells - it took eleven trips. Apart from some help with the foundations and erecting the main frame of the building, Miss Savidge spent the next twenty years reconstructing the house by herself. On her death in 1993, she left the house to her niece, who completed the task.

2. Sea Bank and Lifeboat Station

The sea bank, which is about one mile long, was built in 1859 by the Holkham Estate completing the reclamation of 800 hectares of saltmarsh north-west of Wells, a process which began in 1639. The bank confined the main channel which once meandered through the saltmarshes. The Royal National Lifeboat Institution (RNLI) lifeboat station at the end of the bank, on the beach, houses an all-weather lifeboat and an inshore lifeboat. The first lifeboat at Wells arrived in 1830 and was provided by the Norfolk Shipwreck Association. In 1869, operation of the lifeboat was taken over by the RNLI, who constructed a new lifeboat house at the west end of the quay. In 1895, a replacement lifeboat house was built on Wells beach. In 1936, Wells was the last lifeboat station in Britain to use horses to launch a lifeboat.

3. Holkham National Nature Reserve

Holkham Nature Reserve covers an area of about 3706 hectares (9158 acres) from Wells to Burnham Overy. It comprises a number of habitats including saltmarshes, sand dunes, woodland, beach and fresh water grazing marshes. The woodland area of Corsican, Maritime and Scots pine was planted during the second half of the nineteenth century by the second Earl of Leicester to stabilise the dunes and allow land to be reclaimed for agricultural use. After World War II, this land reverted to fresh water grazing.

4. Holkham Village

Like other parishes in this part of Norfolk, Holkham originally had two settlement areas, one, Holkham Town, was on the site now occupied by Holkham Hall and the other, Holkham Staithe, is now known as Holkham village. The village, as it appears today, seems to be a typical estate village, with the late Victorian semi-detached cottages and a reading room, which gives an appropriate look to the northern approach to the Hall. The partial remodelling of the village in the late nineteenth century hides the fact that, for many centuries, it had been a typical village of owner/occupiers and tenants. At least one building, the Ancient House, dates to the sixteenth century and others have been occupied since the eighteenth century. Not all the houses in the village were in keeping with the new Hall and model farms being built on the estate, indeed some were regarded as so dilapidated as to be a danger to life. So, in addition to building new houses, the Cokes gradually purchased existing ones, subsequently demolishing and rebuilding them to give the village a more uniform look.

5. The Monument

As you walk back towards Wells along the coast path or up Lady Anne's Drive towards Holkham Park, you can see the Monument rising above the trees. This 37 metre (120 feet), Corinthian column was erected as a memorial to the agricultural improver Thomas William Coke (1754-1842).

Designed by William Danthorne (1799-1859), it was paid for by public subscription and erected 1845-8. The plinth on which the column stands is 44 feet square; on three sides there are depictions of the improving work of Coke of Norfolk - sheep shearing, irrigation and the granting of long leases, while the north side carries the dedication. At the corners of the plinth are sculptures of an ox, a sheep, a plough and a seed drill. The column is surmounted by a drum supporting a sheaf of corn.

6. Arch House

Arch House, Mill Road, Wells is a three storey house built in the late eighteenth century. It is now run as bed and breakfast accommodation.

Notes about walk

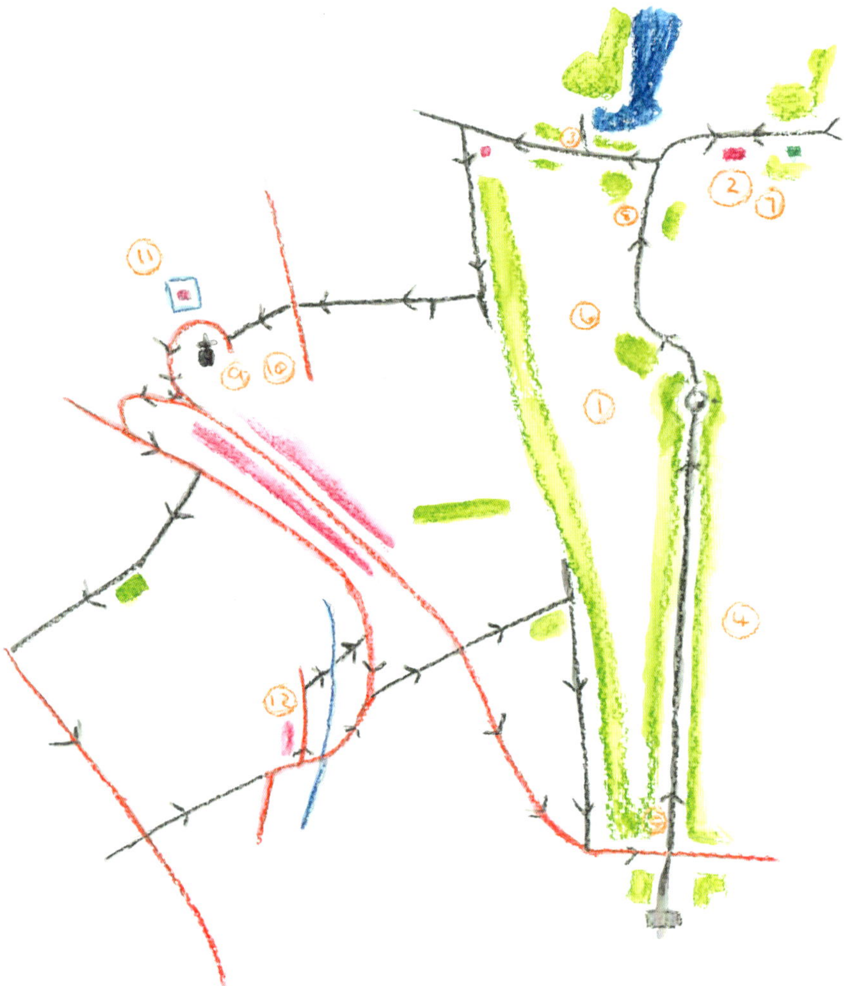

Walk 7: *Holkham to Burnham Thorpe*

Summary

The walk uses well made estate roads, country lanes as well as footpaths, bridleways and tracks. The walking is relatively easy, although there is some uneven ground and some steep inclines to negotiate. The landscape varies from country house parkland to open arable fields with distant views to the coast and surrounding villages and some woodland walking. It is a long walk and an alternative shorter route is included.

The Route

Distance: 12½ miles.
Time: 4/4½ hours.
Suggested car park: Holkham Hall main car park, Holkham Park, NR23 lRH TF 8880 4295
Map Sheet: OS Explorer 251

1. Leave the car park heading westwards (left) and walk towards Holkham Hall. Follow the road as it bends sharply to the left by the lake.

2. At the fork in the road, turn right and follow the road to the gate and the cattle grid.

3. Go through the gate and follow the road as it climbs towards the woodland and the West Lodge beyond.

4. At the West Lodge, go through the gate leaving the park and turn immediately left (following the Lodge garden wall) and continue along the bridleway.

5. After approximately ¾ mile, take the bridleway (first track to the right), and head towards the field barn. Continue along this path until you reach the road. There are distant views towards the sea from this path.

6. Cross the road with care and continue along the path as it descends towards Burnham Thorpe. Where the path becomes a tarmac road, follow the road, between the church and a moated manor house, towards the village.

7. At the fork in the road, go right and head towards the junction.

8. At the T junction, turn right (signed Burnham Market) and continue along the road to the next junction.

9. At the T junction, turn left and follow the road towards Burnham Thorpe. Immediately after the speed limit sign, take the track to the right (signed as a footpath), and ascend Gravel Pit Hill. Go left by the barn and continue towards the woodland.

10. Go right and follow the path along the edge of the wood. If you pause for a moment here, there are distant views to the right of Burnham Overy tower mill, Burnham Market and the sea beyond. Behind you are views back to Burnham Thorpe.

11. Continue along this path as it descends towards the B1355.

12. At the road, turn left and walk for approximately ½ mile. Care should be taken on this busy road.

13. After approximately ½ mile, turn left (crossing the road with care) and follow the track towards Burnham Thorpe.

14. At the road, turn left and continue towards the village.

15. At the fork in the road, go left (signed Burnham Thorpe) and continue to the site of the Old Parsonage.*

** Alternative route: Horses roam freely over the meadow on either side of the River Burn. For an alternative route, turn right here over the bridge and follow the road for approximately ¼ mile until you reach the bridleway on the right, then follow main route (19)*

16. At the Old Parsonage site, turn right and follow the footpath across meadow to the footbridge.

17. Cross the footbridge over the River Burn and head across the meadow to the gate, go through the gate to the road.

18. At the road, turn right and continue until you reach the bridleway to the left.

19. Both routes: Follow the bridleway to the road.**

*** For a shorter walk back, turn right on the road and continue until you reach the bridleway at the edge of Holkham Park. Follow the main route from here. (24)*

20. Cross the road and continue along the bridleway as it ascends towards Holkham Park. At the top there are 360° views of the surrounding countryside.

21. Ignore the path to the left, and continue to the hedge.

22. Follow the path, keeping the hedge on your left (signed public footpath). Go left as it follows the edge of some woodland and continue until you reach the wall surrounding Holkham Park.

23. At the Park wall, turn right. Keep the wall to your left and follow the path until you reach the road.

24. At the road turn left. Both routes: follow the Park wall to the South Lodge.

25. At the South Lodge, turn left and re-enter Holkham Park. Take a moment here to look back across the road to the Triumphal Arch.

26. Follow the avenue to the Obelisk.

27. Walk around the Obelisk, go through the gate and continue following the road as it descends towards Holkham Hall and the car park.

Points of Interest

1. Holkham Park

At eleven square kilometres, Holkham Park is the largest country house park in Norfolk. As a designed landscape it is of national importance. First appearances would suggest it was the creation of a single individual working to a single design. The reality is somewhat different, the development of Holkham Park is long and complex and involved some of the most important names in landscape design, for example Lancelot 'Capability' Brown (1716-1783) and Humphrey Repton (1752-1818). Work on creating a suitable setting for the new house began before work on the house itself commenced; planting in Obelisk Wood began in 1720s and 1730s. As originally conceived, the woods, avenues, and vistas had a more formal, geometric design; these were gradually softened until by the early nineteenth century the landscape had a more fashionable naturalistic look. The lake was created by damming a natural watercourse, it was given a serpentine 'twist' at the northern end in 1789 and one at the southern end in 1803. One of the most significant changes in the park's development was its increase in size. In 1759, when Thomas Coke died, the park covered about 150 hectares (370 acres). After the accession of Thomas William Coke (1754-1842) in 1776, it was expanded, until by 1800 the park covered 1200 hectares (2965 acres). The expansion took place in all directions, but mostly to the south. One unusual feature of the park is the fact that land to the south of Obelisk Wood is arable rather than pasture, reflecting Thomas William Coke's interest in agricultural improvement.

Between 1833 and 1839 a nine mile long perimeter brick wall was constructed around the park. Its exact purpose is unclear; its height makes it unlikely to keep game birds in the park or to keep unwelcome visitors out. It is the longest park wall in East Anglia.

2. Holkham Hall

Holkham Hall is a large country house built in the Palladian style, owned by the Coke family, Earls of Leicester. The origins of the family fortune lay in the law, with the Elizabethan/Jacobean lawyer Sir Edward Coke (1552-1634), who was the first holder of the title Lord Chief Justice of England. He first purchased land in Holkham in 1612 and this property has remained in the Coke family ever since, although not always passing by direct descent.

Like many country houses built in the eighteenth century, Holkham Hall was designed not by one individual, but by a group of men; the owner Thomas Coke (1697-1759) 1st Earl of Leicester, his friend Lord Burlingham (1694-1753) an enthusiast for the Palladian style, the architect Matthew Brettingham (1699-1769) and William Kent (c.1685-1748). In 1714, while in Rome on the Grand Tour, Thomas Coke developed an interest in art and architecture which remained with himself for the rest of his life, and ultimately led to the creation of Holkham Hall.

Thomas Coke inherited Holkham at the age of ten years, after the death of his father. Instead of going to University, in 1712, Coke, at the age of fifteen years, was sent on a Grand Tour of Europe. The Grand Tour was intended to widen the cultural and social horizons of those who undertook it and usually lasted two-three years, Thomas Coke returned in 1718, after nearly double that time. While in Europe, he formed a friendship with William Kent and as a result of that friendship, an interest in art. Kent went on to purchase paintings in Italy on Coke's behalf. Holkham Hall was designed to house the collection of paintings and classical sculptures Coke brought back from his Grand Tour.

3. The Walled Garden

The Walled Garden was constructed in the 1780s and includes a 30.4 metres (100 feet) long vinery, designed by Samuel Wyatt (1737-1807). The 4.2 metres (14 feet) high walls enclose approximately 3 hectares (7 acres) of garden with a 1 hectare orchard to the south. The garden is divided into eight areas, some of which retain their nineteenth century glasshouses and cold frames. There is a vast glasshouse built in 1872, which has been fully restored.

4. South Avenue

The South Avenue runs for three kilometres from the Triumphal Arch (designed by William Kent in 1739, but not completed until 1752) to the Obelisk (designed by William Kent in 1730), which stands on the highest point in the park. The stone Obelisk

is 25 metres (80 feet) tall.
The purpose of the Triumphal Arch was to announce the approach of the house for those arriving from the south, and to symbolise the influence of the house beyond the park walls.

5. Longlands

Longlands Farm, together with the Great Barn, was the site of the famous Sheep Shearings, three day summer gatherings, which began in the 1790s and continued until 1821. These were the forerunners of the modern county agricultural shows. At these gatherings, the latest improvements in arable techniques and animal husbandry were shared among the house guests and visitors.

6. The Temple

The Temple (in Obelisk Wood) was designed by William Kent.

7. Perseus and Andromeda Fountain

The Perseus and Andromeda fountain (originally called St George and the Dragon) was designed by C. R. Smith and exhibited at the Great Exhibition of 1851. When running, the fountain uses 400 gallons (1818 litres) of water per minute. It was fed from a reservoir at the top of the deer park which held sufficient water for the fountain to run for only twenty minutes at a time. The water would then have to be pumped back up to the reservoir to allow the fountain to run again. In 2009, some of the corroded iron water pipes failed and the fountain ceased working until 2015. A restoration programme begun that year included installing equipment which allows for the recirculation of water from the bowl of the fountain, thus allowing it to run for longer.

8. The Ice House

The thatched Ice House is a survival from the previous house and dates from the late seventeenth century

9. Burnham Thorpe

Burnham Thorpe is another long established village. The earliest datable archaeological finds are Neolithic flint axe heads. It was mentioned in the Domesday Book of 1086. The village lies in the valley of the River Burn, from which it derives part of its name, the other part, thorpe, is an old Norse word for farmstead. During the medieval period the settlement had two churches All Saints' and St Peter's, which no longer exists, but once stood to the west of the present church. The Lord Nelson public house is a seventeenth century building originally called The Plough. It was named in Nelson's honour after the Battle of the Nile in 1798. Nelson returned infrequently to the village, but he did live there from 1788-1793, when held in reserve on half-pay, and it is known he frequented The Plough.

10. All Saints' Church

All Saints' Church dates from the thirteenth century, with some remodelling in the fourteenth and fifteenth centuries. There was a partial tower collapse in the nineteenth century. The church was renovated in the 1840s and completely restored in 1905, in time for the centenary of the Battle of Trafalgar. The church contains some items of Nelsoniana. The church has a white pre-1801 style ensign.

11. The Manor House

The Manor House is possibly seventeenth century with eighteen and nineteenth century alterations, surrounded by a moat that is possibly medieval.

12. Site of the Old Parsonage

Admiral Horatio Nelson (1758-1805) was born in the village in 1758 and was baptised in the church where his father, Edmund Nelson, was Rector from 1755-1803. The old parsonage where Nelson was born no longer exists, it was demolished in 1803 shortly after Edmond Nelson's death. A replacement was built nearby and is now a private house.

Notes about walk

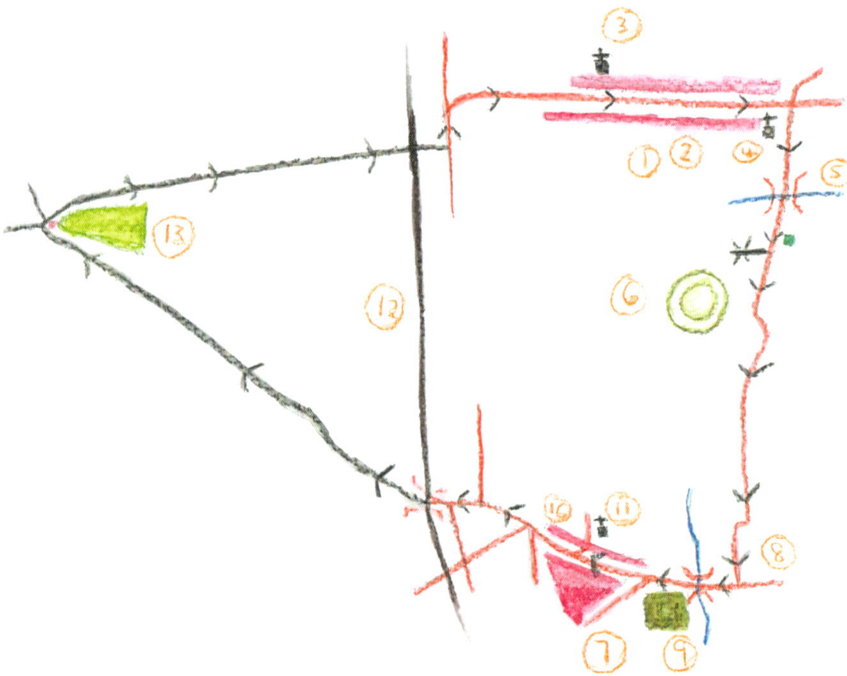
3
1
2
4
5
13
12
6
10
11
8
7
9

Walk 8: *Warham and Wighton*

Summary

This walk around the villages of Warham and Wighton uses country lanes and rough tracks. There are some inclines but the walk is generally relatively easy. It crosses the River Stiffkey and the Wells and Walsingham Light Railway twice. At the start of the walk there is a short detour to an ancient site, Warham Camp, some 2000 years old. It then meanders through Wighton before climbing to Gallows Hill wood, where the track swings back towards Warham. This section of the walk provides pleasant views to the coast (north wards) and to undulating arable fields to the south. The route then winds its way through the village of Warham, back to the car park.

The Route

Distance: 5¾ miles.
Time: 2/2½ hours.
Suggested car park: Grass verge to the north of Warham Camp.
(NR23 lNJ gives All Saints Church, Warham)
TF 9489 4102
Map Sheet: OS Explorer 251

1. Leave your car and head south for a short distance to the track to Warham Camp. Turn right and take a short detour to visit this Iron Age Fort.

2. Return to the road and turn right and head towards Wighton.

3. At the junction, by Copy's Green Farm, turn right and walk to Wighton, crossing the bridge over the River Stiffkey.

4. Continue along the High Street until you reach the junction.

5. At the junction, turn right (signed Wells), then almost immediately, at the bend turn left (signed 'Unsuitable for motor vehicles'). The road crosses the Well and Walsingham Light Railway (WWLR) and passes Wighton cemetery.

6. After a short distance the tarmac road becomes a track; follow this track as it winds its way between arable fields and eventually climbs towards Gallow Hill Wood.

7. At Cuckoo Lodge, ignoring all other tracks, walk around the boundary of the garden and turn eastwards towards Warham.

8. Follow the track back to the road at Warham. Take care when crossing the WWLR at the level crossing. The track has sea views to the left and views to the surrounding countryside to the right.

9. At the road, turn left and walk towards the T-junction.

10. At the junction, turn right and walk through Warham village.

11. At the crossroads, by the Three Horse Shoes pub and All Saints' church, turn right (signed Wighton) and follow the road over the River Stiffkey back to your car.

Points of Interest

1. Warham

Warham has a long history of human settlement, with the earliest archaeological finds dating to the Neolithic period. Its name could derive from Old English meaning something like 'a homestead by water or marsh by high ground'. Warham once had three medieval churches', one, St Mary the Virgin, was demolished when the three parishes merged at the time of the Reformation. It stood just to the south of the present day All Saints'. The other two are still in use. The village has a number of former Holkham Estate cottages (for example, Long Acre 26, The Street and the Lodge to Warham House built c1840). Church Farmhouse was built 1801/3 and was designed by Samuel Wyatt for the Earl of Leicester. Number 29-31, The Street is the former Warham All Saints' Public Elementary School. It was built in 1869, enlarged in 1907 and scheduled for closure in 1958/9 and converted into a house.

2. The Reading Room, Warham

The Reading Room (now a village hall) was erected in 1892 at the personal expense of then Rector of Warham, the Reverend Charles Digby, on land given by the Earl of Leicester. Reading Rooms were popular in the late

Victorian period, they provided a place where adults could learn to read and write. With the introduction of compulsory education for children, this need began to decline and many were converted into village halls.

3. Church of St Mary Magdalene, Warham

St Mary Magdalene possibly has a Saxo-Norman tower but dates mainly to the fourteenth century. It has Norwich and foreign stained glass dating from the fifteenth to the nineteenth centuries. In 1800-1 the interior was remodelled. It is now a chapel of ease.

4. All Saints' Church, Warham

All Saints' is the present day parish church and dates to circa 1300, with later additions. It is relatively small in size, but was once much larger: the aisles and tower have been demolished. The church was restored in the 1870s and again in the 1890s. In the Chancel, there is a memorial to the man largely responsible for the restorations, Charles Tilton Digby, Rector of Warham 1874-1923. The church has an alabaster reredos depicting the Last Supper and stained glass window above dating from the 1890s restoration.

5. Bridge over the River Stiffkey

The bridge over the River Stiffkey was built in 1812. From the bridge you can see the park-like landscape of the former Warham Old Hall, a

Tudor manor house. In 1709, the estate was purchased by the Turners, a family of merchants from King's Lynn, then in 1785 it was acquired by Coke of Norfolk. The house was demolished shortly afterwards when the land was merged with the Holkham Estate.

6. Warham Camp

There are five Iron Age hillforts in Norfolk, all concentrated in the west of the county: Narborough, Thetford, Holkham, South Creake and Warham. Warham Camp is probably the finest Iron Age earthworks in Eastern England. Unlike a classic hillfort, which usually occupies high ground, Warham, like other forts in Norfolk, is located in a river valley. This location may have been chosen to enable control of a river crossing and its accompanying trade. Roughly circular in form, it differs from other forts in that it does not follow the contours of the land. Excavations of the site, in 1914 and 1959, showed evidence of a timber palisade and a platform at the rear and a timber revetment on the inner face. The exact function of the site is not known, indeed it may not have had a single use and it may not have been in permanent occupation. Possible uses include as a place of refuge in times of trouble or distress, an assembly place for religious or trading purposes, for display, to enhance the prestige of the local community and offer reassurance while at the same time impressing visitors. The fort lies close to a barrow at Fiddlers Hill. It is possible the site was occupied by the Iceni. It is now an SSSI. The chalk grassland is home to wildflowers, insects and butterflies.

Settlement in the area continued after the Iron Age. Since 1951, there have been numerous finds from Warham Roman Settlement, including floor tiles, flue tiles, pottery sherds, and buckles.

7. Wighton

Wighton is also a settlement with a long history. The earliest archaeological finds date to the Neolithic period. The name Wighton derives from Old English possibly meaning 'farm near a village'. It was mentioned in the Domesday Book of 1086. Wighton is home to two Iron Age Forts, although neither exist above ground level today. In 1957/8, a cropmark was excavated which revealed Copy's Green Iron Age Fort. The presence of Roman artifacts suggest the site was re-occupied by the Romans between AD75-200. Wighton Camp, which was known to have existed in the eighteenth/nineteenth centuries, was rediscovered and partly excavated in 1974. The excavation showed evidence of Iron Age and Roman occupation of the site. In 1976, evidence for a Roman pottery kiln was found. In the Roman period, Wighton was part of a settlement which stretched across Walsingham and Wighton. Evidence of a temple and bathhouse have been found. The finds predominantly date to the second to fourth centuries. In contrast to the wealth of material from the Iron Age and Roman period, there is very little Saxon archaeology in Wighton.

As with Warham a number of properties in Wighton were or are part of the Holkham Estate, for example 11 and 12 Copy's Green are early nineteenth estate cottages. Hall Farm was built 1803-6 and designed by Samuel Wyatt.

8. Copy's Green Farmhouse

Copy's Green Farmhouse dates from the seventeenth to nineteenth centuries and has a Doric porch.

9. Wighton Common

Wighton Common, off the High Street, is wet marsh grassland and is home to barn owls, red kite, ragged robin, Lady's Bedstraw and Meadow Sweet.

10. The School House Gallery

The School House Gallery was built in 1873 as the village school, a three roomed building with a teacher's house attached. It was scheduled for closure in 1949/50 and is now an art gallery.

11. All Saints' Church, Wighton

All Saints' church dates to the fourteenth and fifteenth century. The fourteen century tower collapsed in 1965 and was replaced in 1975. The rebuilding was paid for by a Canadian engineer and businessman, Leeds Richardson, whose ancestors are buried in the churchyard. It has fifteenth stained glass windows in the north and south aisles.

12. Wells and Walsingham Light Railway

The Wells and Walsingham Light Railway runs on four miles of the old Great Eastern Railway line from Wells to Walsingham. It was built by Roy Francis and began running services in 1982. It is the longest 10.25 inch narrow gauge railway in the world.

13. Gallows Hill Wood

Gallows Hill, Wells was probably, as its name suggests, the site of a gallows. Nothing is visible today.

Notes about walk

5
6
8
9
1
7
3
2
10
11
4
12
8

Walk 9: *Around the Burnhams*

Summary

This walk uses country lanes, footpaths and sea banks. There are some inclines and uneven ground. The walk starts in the bustling village of Burnham Market, then makes its way to Burnham Norton. Here arable fields give way to reed beds and salt marsh, It leaves the marshes and continues to Burnham Overy Staithe, where a short detour will take you down to the staithe. The walk then climbs through arable fields to Burnham Overy Town and then to Burnham Market.

The Route

Distance: 4 miles.
Time: 1½/2 hours.
Suggested car park: Foundry Place, North Street, Burnham Market.
PE31 8HG
Map Sheet: OS Explorer 251
Alternative car parking: Limited off road parking in Burnham Norton and Burnham Overy Staithe

1. Leave the car park and walk along Foundry Place to the junction.

2. At the junction, turn right into North Street and follow this road to the Market Place.

3. At the Market Place, turn right into Herring Lane. Follow this road as it climbs out of the village.

4. Continue following this road as it descends the hill towards Burnham Norton. Ignore paths to the right and left. There is a view here of Burnham Overy tower mill and watermill.

5. After about 400 feet, turn left and follow the footpath down to the road.

6. Cross the road with care and continue into Burnham Norton (signed Norton Street).

7. Continue along the street passing Norton Hall and the Gilbert Scott Library (an old telephone box).

8. Go right with the road, ignoring the path to the left, and continue straight ahead (signed Burnham Circular Walk).

9. Go right through the opening by the gate. Follow the path through the reed beds and marshland.

10. Continue along this path as it goes left and heads towards the sea defence bank.

11. Climb up the bank and go right (signed Norfolk Coast Path). Cross the bridge and head towards the field.

12. At the hedge, cross the field towards the far hedge, keeping Burnham Overy tower mill to your right).

Here you can make a detour to see Burnham Overy watermill. Take the footpath to the right and walk to the mill, return the same way to continue the walk.

13. At the hedge, turn left and follow the footpath into Burnham Overy Staithe.

(For a shorter walk to Burnham Overy Town, at the field opening cross the road and take the track (signed Restricted Byway) and rejoin the route at (17)

14. At the end of the path, go through the hedge and turn left, follow the road into Burnham Overy Staithe.

15. At the staggered crossroads, you can turn left and take a short detour to the staithe. Return the same way.

16. Cross the road with care and turn right into New Road. Continue along this road as it climbs out of the village. There are panoramic views from this road.

17. As the road descends towards Burnham Overy Town, the alternative route joins the main route from the right.

18. Both routes: follow the road as it enters Burnham Overy Town, with the church and houses to the right.

19. At the junction, turn right (signed Burnham Market). This is a busy road, cross the road with care and walk along the pavement.

20. Cross the River Burn, with Union Mills on your left. Continue along this road into Burnham Market.

21. Continue along this road, ignoring the road to the left (signed Fakenham) and the road to the right (signed Brancaster).

22. Turn right into Foundry Place and walk back to the car park.

Points of Interest

1. Burnham Market

Burnham Market is one of five settlements in the area with the name Burnham (the others are Burnham Norton, Burnham Overy (Staithe and Town) and Burnham Deepdale. Burnham Market resulted from the merger of Burnham Sutton, Burnham Westgate and Burnham Ulph. The earliest evidence for settlement in the area comes from a number of Neolithic axe heads found locally. Burnham derives from Old English meaning a 'village on a stream'. During the Saxon period, Burnham was a place of some importance, probably the centre of a large estate, which eventually broke up to form the different manors and settlements which exist today. From the middle Saxon period, it became a market or trading centre; the market was discontinued some time before 1854. In the Domesday Book of 1086, Burnham Market is indistinguishable from the other Burnhams.

The village originally had five churches, St Andrew's, and St Edmund's Westgate (nothing of which remains), St Ethelbert's Burnham Sutton (which is in ruins), All Saints' Burnham Ulph, and St Mary's Westgate.

Burnham Market was on the West Norfolk Joint Railway line which ran to Wells-next-the-sea. It was opened in 1866, passenger services ended in 1952 and the line was damaged in the 1953 flood. Freight continued between Heacham and Burnham Market until 1964.

Originally called Polstede Hall (designed by Matthew Brettingham in 1750), Burnham Westgate Hall was remodelled in the Palladian Style in 1783-85 by Sir John Soane, for Thomas Pitt, 1st Baron Camelford (1737-1793), the nephew of the Prime Minister, William Pitt the Elder. It was Soane's first major commission for a country house. Thomas Pitt, an amateur architect, had become friends with Soane while on the Grand Tour. It is set in a small park of about 30 acres. In the 1930s and 1940s, it was used by the Women's Section of the Royal British Legion to train domestic servants, before being purchased by Norfolk County Council in 1945, as a residential home for the elderly. The Council sold it in 1990, when it became a private house once more.

2. Foundry House and Satchell's shop

Foundry House is an eighteenth century house with a shop front, in gault brick with early nineteenth century cast iron architectural details from Burnham Market Foundry.

3. Market House and Limetree Cottage

Market House and Limetree Cottage, on the corner of Herring Lane - was built in 1680 and heightened by one storey in about 1720. It has a wooden porch with Tuscan Doric columns and a triangular pediment.

4. St Mary's Church Westgate

St Mary's church is one of the oldest buildings in Burnham Market. Heavily restored in 1872, some original features remain. The tower dates to about 1310 and has rare tower battlement sculpture which dates to about 1500. Other parts of the church date from the fourteenth and fifteenth centuries. The east window was designed in 1953.

5. Burnham Norton

A long established settlement dating back to the Neolithic period. Its name is Old English, meaning something like 'village on a stream with a north farm'. One of the oldest surviving buildings is St Margaret's church, which dates from the fourteenth and fifteenth centuries, with a Saxon round tower. It has a rood screen dating from 1458, which is defaced. Also, there are wall paintings above the Chancel arch and east end of the north aisle.

Richard Woodgett (1845 -1928), master of the sailing clipper Cutty Sark from 1885-1895, was the son of a Burnham Norton farmer. He first went to sea on coasters plying the east coast of Britain and received his master's certificate in 1868 at South Shields. He worked for Jock Willis Shipping Line, owners of the Cutty Sark. A well respected seaman and man manager, he had an affinity with Cutty Sark, getting speeds from the ship not achieved by others. Cutty Sark was built in 1869, for Jock Willis, and was one of the last tea clippers to be built and one of the fastest. The opening of the Suez Canal allowed steam ships to take the shorter route to China, so Cutty Sark spent only a few years on the tea trade, before moving to the wool trade from Australia. Woodgett made several record breaking passages between Britain and Australia. The ship was recorded as travelling 2164 nautical miles in six days. In 1889, the logbook of the SS Britannia records that when steaming at 15-16 knots she was overtaken, at night, by a sailing ship doing 17 knots; the sailing ship turned out to be Cutty Sark. The maximum recorded speed for Cutty Sark was 17.5 knots. On retiring, Richard Woodgett bought a farm at Burnham Overy Staithe. He died in 1928 and was buried in the churchyard of St Margaret's, Burnham Norton.

6. Norton Hall Farm

Norton Hall Farm is a seventeenth century house with eighteenth and nineteenth century alterations.

7. St Mary's Friary, Burnham Norton

St Mary's Friary was the first Carmelite friary established in Norfolk, following the order's departure from Mount Carmel in Palestine in 1238. It was founded by Ralph Hempnale and William Calethorpe in 1242, at Bradmer to the east of Burnham Norton adjacent to the marshes and moved to this site in 1253. The friary was enlarged in 1298 and again in 1353. In 1505, there were between fifteen and seventeen friars living on the site, including the prior and novices. Robert Bale, who died in 1503, was a Carmelite scholar who wrote a history of the order and was a prior at St Mary's at the end of the fifteenth century. In 1537, two Carmelites from Burnham were among those arrested for involvement in a planned uprising against Henry VIII; one of them, John Peacock, was executed at King's Lynn. When the friary was dissolved in 1538 there were only four friars remaining. The buildings and the land were sold to Lady Anne Calthorpe in 1554 and later passed to a branch of the Pepys family, relatives of Samuel, who lived locally. In the eighteenth century, the church was still being used as a farm building but only the gatehouse, west gable end of the church and part of the perimeter wall, together with earthworks, remain. The gatehouse was partly rebuilt and reroofed in the nineteenth century. Friary Cottage, an eighteenth century building with twentieth century alterations, contains the remains of a medieval building which could have been the infirmary or guest hall of the friary.

Springs at the foot of the escarpment north east of the site provided the friary with a water supply. Local tradition identifies one of these as a holy well or wishing well and is recorded on old editions of OS maps as 'Our Lady's Well'.

8. Burnham Overy

Burnham Overy has two distinct settlement areas, Burnham Overy Town (the smaller of the two settlements) and Burnham Overy Staithe. The former is adjacent to the church and the latter on the edge of the marsh. The settlements have a long history, the earliest datable archaeological finds are two Mesolithic flint axes. Fragments of Roman pottery have also been found suggesting a Roman farmstead east of Burnham Overy Staithe. During the medieval period, ships were able to navigate up the River Burn to Burnham Overy Town. As the river silted up, Burnham Overy Staithe developed as the port. Many of the buildings in Burnham Overy are constructed of an unusual building material for North Norfolk, chalk. The reason for this is probably the two large chalk pits found in the area.

9. Burnham Overy Tower Mill

Burnham Overy tower mill was built about 1814 and is a black tarred brick structure, with an onion cap. It stopped working as a mill in about 1922, and was converted into a dwelling in 1926. It was acquired by the National Trust in 1958, restored in the 1980s and is now let as a holiday home. The nearby watermill dates from about 1795 and is attached to the bridge over the River Burn. It was worked by Edward Savory, who also ran the tower mill. It was expanded in 1820 to include a maltings, granary and kiln. From the mid-nineteenth century, the milling machinery was powered by steam rather than water. The building was damaged in the 1953 flood and gutted by fire in 1959. Most of the interior and roof dates to the restoration of the 1960s. It has been owned by the National Trust since 1939 and has been converted to residential use.

10. St Clement's Church Burnham Overy

St Clement's church is very different from almost any other church in Norfolk. It was originally a cruciform building with a central Norman tower. All that remains of the transepts is part of the south transept, which has been used as a vestry. The south aisle and porch remain. The tower has been reduced in height. After the Reformation the tower was blocked off and the nave became the parish church. The chancel had various uses including that of village school. Since 2016, the area beneath the tower has been used as a vestry with toilets and a kitchenette.

11. Union Mills

Union Mills (formerly known as Town Mill and sometimes known as Roy's Mill) is a watermill dating from 1737 and an adjacent tower mill dating from 1814. The watermill was originally two storeys, a third was added in about 1814 and a weatherboarded extension was added about 1820. A miller's house, attached to the watermill, dates to 1737, with extensions in 1744 and 1814. The windmill originally had five floors, a sixth was added later. The watermill's water wheel was undershot; an oil engine was added in

1937. In May 1935, the windmill was gutted by fire. The sails were removed in the twentieth century. In 1953, both mills were flooded to a depth of 2.13 metres (7 feet). The mills had stopped working by 1969 and were sold for conversion to residential use in the late 1990s.

12. All Saints' Church Burnham Ulph

All Saints' is in a very urban setting, sitting between North Street and Front Street. Sometimes referred to as Sutton church, it is actually more correctly Ulph church. During the late eighteenth century, the then rector, Edmund Nelson, obtained permission to merge the parishes of Burnham Sutton and Burnham Ulph, using Ulph church. St Ethelbert's, Burnham Sutton is now in ruins. A Norman church, All Saints' was remodelled in the fourteenth, fifteenth and nineteenth centuries. One Norman window survives in the south nave. It has no tower, a bell hangs from a bell-cote. Early head corbels (one with its tongue out) support the 1908 roof. The pulpit dates to the eighteenth century.

7
6
5
3
8
2
1
4

Walk 10: *Brancaster*

Summary

This walk begins in the pretty village of Brancaster Staithe. After leaving the A149, it climbs via a country lane, through arable fields and woodland, to Barrow Common from where there are views to the coast. It descends to Brancaster, and the coast road, by tracks and footpaths, crosses the site of a Roman fort and then returns to Brancaster Staithe via a marsh boardwalk.

The Route

Distance: 4¾ miles.
Time: 1½/2 hours.
Suggested car park: Harbour Way, Brancaster Staithe, PE31 8BW
TF 7915 4440
Map Sheet: OS Explorer 250
Alternative car parking: Barrow Common or Beach Road, Brancaster (subject to flooding at high tide).

1. Leave the car park, heading towards the A149.

2. At the junction, turn left and walk towards Burnham Deepdale.

3. At Burnham Deepdale, turn right into Dalegate Lane (just before the church and the filling station). Care should be taken when crossing the A149.

4. Follow the road as it climbs towards the woodland. There are views to the coast behind you.

5. As the road bends to the right, take the path to the right and walk through the trees. Go right, rejoin the road and continue to the junction.

6. At the junction, turn right and enter Barrow Common. Ignoring the footpath (first path to the left), take the second path to the left and follow this path across the common.

7. Just beyond the seat, go right and follow the path to the gate. There are views towards Brancaster and Titchwell from this path.

8. At the end of the path, go around the gate through the gap in the hedge. Follow the path (signed Public Footpath). There are views here to Brancaster and Brancaster Staithe. At low tide it is possible to see the wreck of SS Vina.

9. Follow the path as it turns left (signed Circular Walk). There are views here of Brancaster Golf Course.

10. Ignore the track to the left and continue straight ahead to the road (signed Circular Walk).

11. Cross the road with care, then go through the gate into the site of Roman Branodunum. Beware animals graze this land.

12. Head for the far north west corner and go through the gate onto the track. *Here you can go through the second gate and cross the pasture to the Norfolk Coast Path and turn right to head back to Brancaster Staithe,*

13. Turn left and walk to the road.

14. At the road, turn right and follow the road to Marsh Drive.

15. At Marsh Drive, turn right and follow the road to the gate.

16. Go through the gate and turn right on to the Norfolk Coast Path.

17. Follow the boardwalk back to Brancaster Staithe. Take care as the boardwalk is narrow. There are views here across the reed beds and marshes to the left and the houses of Brancaster to the right.

18. At the end of the path, go through the gate and turn right and then left and follow the path back to Harbour Lane.

Points of Interest

1. Brancaster

Brancaster has a long history of human activity. The earliest datable archaeological finds date to the Palaeolithic period. The name Brancaster derives from Branodunum, the third century Roman fort. It derives from either Old English meaning 'broom camp' or a condensed form of the fort's name which derives from Celtic meaning 'crow foot'. The modern day parish of Brancaster comprises the settlements of Brancaster, Brancaster Staithe and Burnham Deepdale.

St Mary's church, Brancaster is partly twelfth century, but is mainly fourteenth century in date. There is evidence for the re-use of Roman masonry in the church. The church has the remains of a rood screen and a sixteenth century font cover.

Brancaster is famous for its wide expanse of beach which stretches to Titchwell. During the 1950s and 1960s it was considered as a possible location for a launch site for the British Space Programme.

2. Brancaster Staithe

Brancaster Staithe was once a busy port, cargoes carried included coal and grain for the malthouses. By the 1800s trade declined, the fishing industry survived and it is a popular area for pleasure craft. The importance of the malt industry to Brancaster is evident by the fact that it once had the largest malthouse (95 metres long and 9.3 metres wide) built in Britain. The malthouse was built in 1747, using material from the Roman fort, but was demolished in the nineteenth century.

Dial House, formerly the Victory Public House, was probably built in the seventeenth century using material from the Roman fort. It was extended in 1700 and again in the late nineteenth or early twentieth century.

Staithe House, late eighteenth century in date was probably a merchant's house, and is a testament to the past wealth of the area.

3. St Mary's Church Burnham Deepdale

St Mary's church, Burnham Deepdale, has a late Saxon round tower which dates to 1050-1100. The church dates to the fourteenth century, but was restored in 1875 and again in 1898. It retains some medieval stained glass and has a rare Norman font of barnack stone, which has figures depicting the months of the year. The rood figures were designed by Sir Walter Tapper (1861-1935), an architect of the Gothick Revival.

4. Barrow Common

Barrow Common takes its name from the Bronze Age barrow once on the site and covers an area of 33 hectares (c82 acres). It is a mosaic of acid grassland, gorse, heather, bracken scrub, and woodland, as well as disused sand and chalk pits. The common was the site of a World War II radar station from 1940 to 1944. The station personnel were billeted at Valley Farm.

5. Scolt Head Island

Originally believed to have developed from a spit of shingle and sand, Scolt Head Island is now thought to have developed from an offshore shingle ridge about two to three thousand years ago. It is 6.5 kilometres (4 miles) in length and has an area of 737 hectares (1820 acres). Much of the island is in the parish of Burnham Norton. It is accessible from either Burnham Overy Staithe or Brancaster Staithe. The National Trust bought most of the island in 1923. Its management was transferred to the Nature Conservancy Council in 1953. In 1986, it became part of the North Norfolk Coast Site of Special Scientific Interest. It comprises a mixture of habitats; sand dunes, salt marsh, intertidal sand and mud flats and shingle, and supports a variety of wildlife. It is an important breeding site for Sandwich and Little terns and has important populations of Common and Arctic terns. The Warden's House on Scolt Head Island was designed, in 1926, by Edward Thomas Boardman (1862-1950) and is on stilts. It was built for the Norfolk Naturalists Trust (owners of part of the island) and paid for by public subscription. The tall chimney was struck by lightning in 1960 and rebuilt.

6. The Wreck of SS Vina

On the sands to the west of Scolt Head Island is the wreck of SS Vina. The ship was built in 1894 by Ramage and Ferguson, Leith for J T Salvesen of Grangemouth, Scotland and spent most of its life on the East Coast Baltic Trade routes. It was 1021 tons and powered by a triple expansion steam engine with a bronze propeller, capable of 9 knots. In 1940, the Vina was requisitioned, filled with concrete and explosives and taken to Great Yarmouth to act as a blocking ship in case of invasion. In 1943, it was moved to Brancaster, then in 1944 towed further offshore to be used as target practice by the Royal Air Force. During a north westerly gale, the Vina was dragged from its position onto a sand bank at the entrance to Brancaster Staithe Harbour; already full of holes, the ship sank. In 1957, the Vina was sold for scrap and cut into three sections in preparation for its removal. A number of attempts have been made to salvage the ship, as it is a hazard to navigation, but it is considered too expensive to remove the wreck from the beach. In 1968, the bronze propeller was removed and floated across the channel, then dragged up the beach by chains. It is advisable to view the wreck from the beach. Those who walk out to the wreck can easily become cut off by an incoming tide, which races into the channel making it impossible to cross, cutting off access to the beach. The wreck is totally submerged at high tide. Those who find themselves in such a predicament are advised to head east to Scolt Head Island and await rescue.

7. Royal West Norfolk Golf Club

The Royal West Norfolk Golf Club, founded in 1892, is a links course and was laid out by Holcombe Ingleby (1854-1926). A solicitor, Ingleby was the son of Shakespearian scholar Clement Mansfield Ingleby and his wife, Sarah Oakes. He was mayor of King's Lynn in 1909 and again 1919 to 1922. In 1910, Ingleby stood as the Conservative candidate for the borough of Lynn. He won by 97 votes. An election petition was called, due to his generosity with gifts of game and parties given at his home, Sedgeford Hall. The case lasted several days, but the two judges decided the gifts and parties did not amount to corrupt practices. Ingleby remained the MP for King's Lynn until 1918. The club is inaccessible at high tide.

8. Branodunum, Roman Fort

Branodunum, a Roman Fort, was probably constructed between 225 and 250AD, replacing an earlier fort on the same site. It was one of eleven forts built between Brancaster and Porchester, Hampshire. The forts were built at different times; the earliest (Brancaster, Caister-on-Sea and Reculver) may have had more to do with trade than defence. The later forts, like Burgh Castle, probably had a more defensive role, protecting the coast from Barbarian raids. The garrison at Brancaster included units from Gaul (modern day France) and Dalmatia (Croatia/ Bosnia). The fort originally had stone walls but these were demolished in the eighteenth century. Cropmarks indicate the location of internal buildings, and archaeological finds suggests occupation was between the third and fourth centuries. There was a planned Roman Viscus (Romano-British settlement) to the east and west of the fort. A Roman Mosaic has been found in the village.

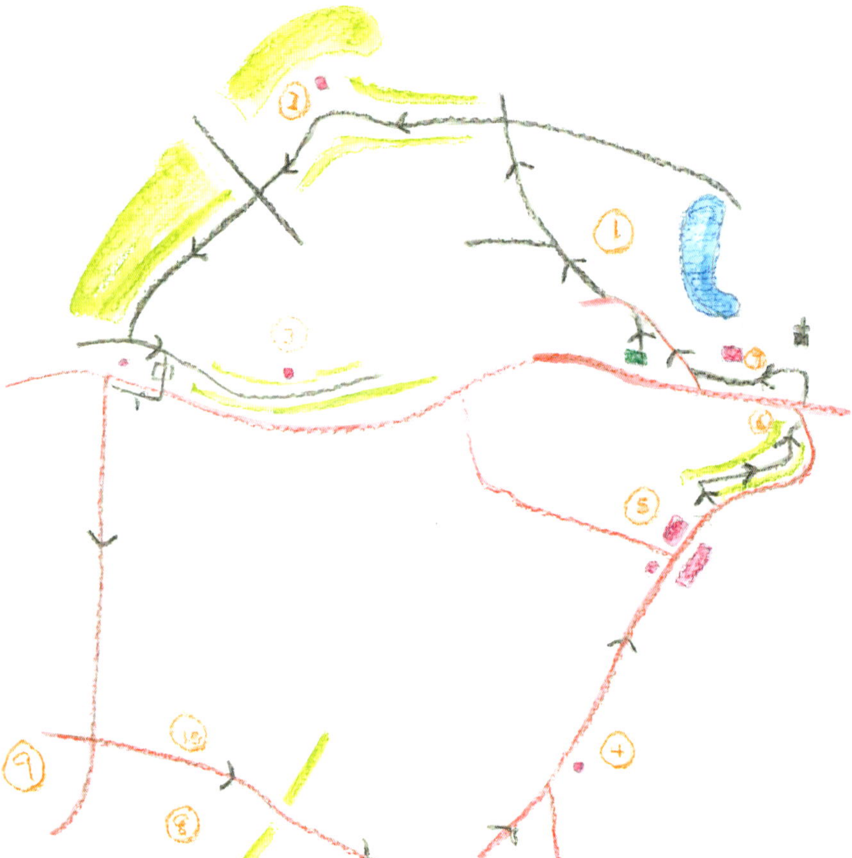

Walk 11: *Around Blickling*

Summary

This route uses well made all purpose tracks, woodland paths and country lanes. The walking is relatively easy, but there are some inclines to negotiate. It begins in parkland setting at Blickling, with views of the house and lake, then moves through woodland out into the arable fields around Oulton Street and the tiny hamlet of Silvergate, before returning to Blickling Park.

The Route

Distance: 5 miles.
Time: 2/2½ hours.
Suggested car park: Main car park, Blickling Estate NRll 6NF
TG 1762 2862
Map Sheet: OS Explorer 252
Alternative car parking: Woodgate Car Park or Bucks Common Car Park

1. From the visiter centre, leave the car park turning left to follow the road to the park gates.

2. Go through the gates and continue straight ahead (signed Weavers Way). As the path gently climbs there are views of the lake. Walk to the gate.

3. Go through the gate and take the path to the left, after a few paces go left again and follow this path towards the woodland. There are fine views across the surrounding landscape from this path.

4. Where two paths meet, turn left, keeping the Mausoleum to your right. Continue along this path towards the path running along the edge of the pasture. At this point the Tower can be seen across the park.

5. At the end of the path, turn right and follow the track as it descends towards Woodgate car park.

6. Before reaching the car park, turn left and follow the path between the pasture and woodland. Continue along this path until you reach the all purpose track.

7. At the track, turn left and head towards Bucks Common car park.

8. Turn right, walk through the car park and, taking care, cross the road, turning right, walk towards the junction.

9. At the junction, turn left and follow New Road towards Oulton Street (signed Oulton Street/Cawston).

10. At the crossroads, turn left and continue towards Abel Heath.

11. At Abel Heath, go left and walk for a short distance before turning left again, passing Abel Heath Farm on your right. Follow the road through Silvergate.

12. Just past the cottages, turn left through the hedge and take the path through the woodland.

13. Go through the gate, cross the pasture heading towards the second gate. Go through this and follow the path through the second piece of woodland. At the end of the path you will see the ice house to your left.

14. Leave the woodland, turn left onto the road and head for the junction.

15. At the junction, taking care, cross the road and enter the churchyard.

16. Follow the path through the churchyard.

17. Leave the churchyard, walk by the main gate of Blickling Hall and follow the path back to the car park.

Points of Interest

1. Blickling Hall and Estate

Blickling is a long established settlement. Its name is Old English meaning the homestead of Blicia. The earliest datable finds are Neolithic axe heads, there is a Bronze Age barrow in the park woodland. Blickling was a Royal Manor given to the Bishops of Thetford after 1066. The Domesday Book mentions several outlying settlements (including Oulton and Hevingham) associated with the manor of Blickling. In the late fourteenth century, the manor was acquired by Sir Nicholas Dagworth, who built a large moated manor house on the site of the present day hall. Thereafter, the house passed through several families including the

Erpinghams (Sir Thomas Erpingham fought at Agincourt with Henry V) and the Boleyns. Anne Boleyn is said to have been born in the house and spent much of her early childhood there; unfortunately, this is a claim made for just about every house the Boleyns ever owned. The Blickling estate is in the parishes of Blickling, Oulton and Itteringham.

In 1605, the manor was acquired by Sir Henry Hobart (pronounced Hubbard 1560-1626) who built the present house. It was designed by Robert Lyminge (architect of Hatfield House) and was constructed between 1618 and 1629. The house passed to Sir John Hobart (1693-1756), created Earl of Buckinghamshire in (1746) and then to the 2nd Earl (also John, 1723-1793) who remodelled the house between 1765 and 1785. Nevertheless, much of the Jacobean interior and layout survives, and it is considered to be one of the finest Jacobean houses in the country. On the 2nd Earl's death, the estate passed to his youngest daughter, Caroline, Lady Suffield (1767-1850). During her tenure, the hall twice escaped destruction by fire, first in 1808 (when the people of Aylsham helped to fight the blaze) and again in 1849 when staff at the hall extinguished the flames. The Suffields had no children and the estate passed to Caroline's elder sister Harriet, and then, in 1850, to her 9 year old nephew William Kerr (pronounced Carr, 1832-1870), 8th Marquess of Lothian. It was bequeathed to the National Trust by Philip Kerr (1882-1940), 11th Marquess of Lothian, on his death in 1940. The house has one of most historically significant collections of books in England. It was created by Sir Richard Ellys (1682-1742) a relative of the Hobarts, and contains over 12,500 volumes. The estate is 1933 hectares (4777 acres) and consists of approximately 200 hectares (500 acres) of woodland, 180 hectares (450 acres) of parkland and 1400 hectares (3500 acres) of farmland.

2. The Mausoleum

The pyramidal Mausoleum was built in 1793 and designed by Joseph Bonomi the elder (1730-1808), a fashionable London architect who had been born in Italy, for Caroline Hobart, Lady Suffield as a burial place, for her father the 2nd Earl of

Buckinghamshire, and his two wives. It is 13.7 metres by 13.7 metres (45 feet by 45 feet).

3. The Tower House

The Tower House was built by Thomas Ivory (1709-1779) and William Ivory in 1773 as a prospect overlooking a nearby race course (to the south of the park) created in the late eighteenth century.

4. Abel Heath Farm

Abel Heath Farm is a seventeenth century house with later alterations and repairs.

5. Silvergate

Silvergate has a number of former estate cottages which date from the seventeenth, eighteenth and nineteenth centuries.

6. The Ice House

The ice house dates from circa 1800.

7. Yew Hedges

The yew hedges flanking the entrance drive to the house are thought to be 300 years old and are approximately 91 metres (300 feet) long and 5.4 metres (18 feet) high. It takes two people two weeks to cut them.

8. Oulton

The name Oulton comes from the Old English meaning 'Outhalt's enclosure'. The earliest datable finds are two flint axe heads from the Mesolithic period. The parish has three settlement areas, Oulton, centred around the church, Oulton Street and Irmingland. St Peter's and St Paul's church dates from circa1350 and is a mixture of decorated and Perpendicular styles and was altered in the eighteenth century. Oulton Hall, which dates to the eighteenth century, was extensively damaged by fire in 2015, but has since been restored. Irmingland Hall is a fragment of a house of 1609, altered in the eighteenth and twentieth centuries.

9. Oulton Airfield

Oulton Airfield was opened in 1940 and was used by both RAF and USAF bomber squadrons. It operated until 1946 and was decommissioned in 1949; some of the buildings remain, including the control tower. Large sections of the runways were removed in 1979 and used as hardcore for the Aylsham by pass. The remaining runways have been used as the foundations for poultry sheds. In 1939, the Blickling estate was requisitioned by the government, parts of Blickling Hall were used as barracks for airmen from the airfield.

10. Wood Farm

Wood Farm dates from 1698.

4
2
8 9
1
10
7
6
5
3

Walk 12: *Sheringham Park and Weybourne*

Summary

This walk uses estate roads, country lanes, footpaths and tracks. There are some inclines and uneven ground. It starts in woodland and pasture of Sheringham Park. During May and June the woodland comes alive with the vivid colour of rhododendrons and azaleas. There are distant views to the coast. Leaving the park, it continues through arable fields to the coast path and the village of Weybourne, from where it climbs back, along country lanes, into Sheringham Park.

The Route

Distance: 6½ miles.
Time: 2½/3 hours.
Suggested car park: Visitors Car Park, Wood Farm, Sheringham Park
NR26 8TL
TG 1385 4114
Map Sheet: OS Explorer 252
Alternative car parking: North Norfolk District Council Car Park, Beach Road , Weybourne.

1. Leave the car park and head towards the visitor centre, take the second left and follow the main avenue to the cattle grid.

2. At the cattle grid, go through the gate and head towards Sheringham Hall.

3. Where the paths meet in front of the Hall, turn left (signed to the gazebo) and head towards the gate.

4. Go through the gate and turn right. Follow the path along the field edge until you reach the road (A149).

5. Take care when crossing the road, go through the hedge and follow the path along the field edge to the hedge.

6. Go through the hedge and turn left, follow the path, over the bridge, to the coast path. The bridge crosses the North Norfolk Railway (NNR).

7. At the cliff top, turn left and follow the coast path towards the old Coastguard cottages. Care should be taken when walking along the coast path. The cliffs in this area are unstable and you should keep away from the cliff edge.

8. Go through the gate and walk past the Coastguard cottages.

9. At the garden boundary, turn right and go through the hedge, follow the path to Weybourne beach car park.

10. Cross the car park and walk along Beach Road into Weybourne village.

11. At the junction, turn left and follow the road as it bends sharply to the right.

12. At the junction (opposite the church), turn right. After a short distance, turn left into Station Road.

13. Follow this road as it bends to the right and then climbs towards Weybourne Station (NNR).

14. Walk over the bridge (take care as there are no pavements on this part of the road), then turn left and follow the track running parallel to the railway line. (If the station is open, it is possible to cross the railway line using the station footbridge).

15. Go through the gate, turn right and climb the steps into Weybourne Heath.

16. Turn right at the top of the steps, follow the path as it skirts the edge of a pit.

17. Continue along the path as it descends the slope, ignore the track to the right.

18. Follow the path as it bends to the right, ignore the path to the left.

19. At the sign 'Visitor Centre and Car Park', turn left.

20. Go through the barrier, continue along the path, ignoring the path to the left.

21. By the pond (on your right), go right, ignoring the path to the left.

22. Where the path forks, take the left fork which climbs steeply away from the path you have just been on.

23. Follow this path to the main avenue.

24. At the main avenue, turn right and follow the path back to the visitor centre and car park.

Points of Interest

1. Sheringham Park, Upper Sheringham

In 1811, Abbot Upcher (1784-1819) and his wife, Charlotte Wilson (1790-1857), purchased the Sheringham estate. A year later, they commissioned Humphrey Repton (1752-1818), together with his son John Adey Repton (1775-1840), to design a house and remodel the park. Sheringham Park was Repton's final project and his favourite. It took a while to finalise the location for the house; sea views were eventually sacrificed for the shelter provided by a low hill. Building began in 1813 and by 1817 the roof was complete. After Abbot Upcher died in 1819, his wife decided not to live in the house. It was only completed in 1839, on the marriage of her son Henry Ramey Upcher (1810-1892). The open pasture area is quite small, less than 35 hectares (86 acres), but there are extensive woodlands; the species and planting of the trees was decided by Upcher rather than Repton. To keep the park private, a public road was closed, one end becoming a main drive to the house. The rhododendrons, for which the park is famous today, were added to the woodland from the 1850s, and increased by Henry Morris Upcher (1839-1921) in the early twentieth century from seed he obtained from the plantsman Ernest 'Chinese' Wilson (1876-1930). The diversity of rhododendron in the collection was improved by Thomas Upcher (1906 -1985), the last owner of Sheringham Park. He would hold rhododendron parties in the park and built two towers to provide his guests with a better view of the display. There are approximately 80 species represented today. Sheringham Park has been owned by the National Trust since 1987, following the death of Thomas Upcher.

To the north-west of the house is Spy Hill, a gazebo (or lookout tower) was first placed there in 1803. A replacement was the victim of arson and by the 1980s was considered unsafe. In 1987, a new gazebo, with a steel frame, was installed. The steel frame was lowered into place by helicopter. It provides panoramic views of both the park and the surrounding countryside.

2. Upper Sheringham

The name Sheringham is Old English meaning the 'homestead of Scira's people'. Until the nineteenth century, Upper Sheringham was the main settlement. Sheringham, on the cliff top, was a collection of fishermen's cottages. Upper Sheringham has a long history dating back to the Neolithic period. The entry in the Domesday Book of 1086 covers both Upper Sheringham and Sheringham. The oldest surviving building in the parish is All Saints' church, dating from the early fourteenth and mid-fifteenth centuries. It has a fourteenth century rood screen and a pulpit and oak reredos by Cecil Upcher FRIBA (1884-1972) and a collection of fifteenth century carved bench ends which depicts, among other things, a cat carrying a kitten in its mouth. On the north wall of the chancel is a memorial to Abbot Upcher, by the sculptors John Bacon (1777-1859) and Samuel Manning (1789-1842).

The Dales was built in 1913-1914, possibly by Edward Boardman, in the style of a late sixteenth century house. Between 1914 and 1918, it was used as a hospital, later it became a care home for the elderly and it is now a hotel.

3. Ivy Lodge, Sheringham Park

Ivy Lodge bears the date 1905, but in fact the house dates back to the early nineteenth century; Repton's Red Book shows a single storey thatched house, with the same plan on this site. The house is also shown on the 1838 Tithe Commutation map. The lodge was rebuilt with two storeys, by Henry Morris Upcher, following a fire.

4. Weybourne

The name Weybourne is Old English and means 'felon's stream', suggesting the area may have been a place where criminals were drowned. It has a long history, a hoard of 206 Iron Age coins have been found in the village.

5. Weybourne Mill

Weybourne Mill was built in the mid-nineteenth century, it is five storeys high and was last used to grind grain in 1916. In about 1920, the mill and attached granary were converted for residential use by J S Brockleby, an Arts and Craft architect. Local folklore says, the miller would stop the sails in the sign of a cross as a warning to smugglers of the presence of customs men.

6. Old Coastguard Cottages

The Coastguard Cottages are perched on cliffs 40 feet high and have a commanding view of this stretch of coast line. The duty room is the section of the building nearest the cliff edge and was originally reached by an external stairs.

7. All Saints' Church and Weybourne Priory

The Augustinian Priory of the Blessed Virgin and All Saints' was founded in the twelfth or early thirteenth century by Sir Ralph Mainwaring.

Initially, it was subordinate to the priory at West Acre. Following a dispute in 1314, the canons at Weybourne were allowed to elect their own prior, in return for paying a small pension to West Acre. It was founded for seven canons, but never had more than four in the fifteenth century. In 1514, it was said the priory could not financially support more than two. When it was suppressed in 1536, there was a prior, one canon and three other persons living in the monastery. Spring Beck provided a water supply for the monastery. Part of the ruins, including the cloisters, lay in a neighbouring garden.

The Augustians took over the site of an earlier building, incorporating the existing church into the monastic church. A part of its ruined central tower still remains today. The church was enlarged to meet the needs of the monastery and the parish. All Saints' church dates from the thirteenth century, the porch and tower were completed in the fourteen century. The porch originally incorporated a wayfarers' chapel. The church was restored in the nineteenth century. The pulpit has early seventeenth panels from a three decker pulpit.

8. Weybourne Spring Hotel

In the late 1890s, there were attempts to develop Weybourne as an exclusive holiday resort. The Weybourne Spring Hotel, located beyond the road bridge next to Weybourne station, was a product of this ambition. Built by the owner of a local gravel pit, it was opened in 1903 and had 36 guest rooms. It was similar in style to the Links Hotel at West Runton. As a hotel it had a checkered history, by 1910 it had ceased trading, but was in use again in the 1920s, closing for good by 1929. It became a residential care home for disabled people. The building was demolished about 1939, a myth developed that the reason for demolition was to prevent such a prominent building becoming a landmark for enemy bombers. The truth is more prosaic, the hotel was built on light sandy ground and its foundations began to fail, making the building unstable; it was demolished to prevent its collapse.

9. Weybourne Station

The North Norfolk Railway (NNR) is a heritage line running from Sheringham to Holt. It operates on part of the route of the former M&GNJR line from Norwich to Cromer via Holt. The section from Norwich to Melton Constable was opened in 1884 and that from Holt to Cromer in 1887. The line closed in 1964. NNR re-opened the Sheringham to Weybourne section in 1970 and from Weybourne to Holt in the 1980s. When the line was originally built there was no station at Weybourne, the line runs over a mile away from the village. The station appears to have been built at the request of the owners of the Weybourne Spring Hotel. The station was opened to passengers in 1901 and is not typical of a M&GNJR station and was one of the grandest on the network.

10. Saw Mill, Sheringham Wood

The saw mill, Sheringham Wood, was originally powered by a portable steam engine. It was built about 1927, by Dening of Chard, Somerset. Wood was fed to the saw blade by rail. It was used to provide timber for maintenance on the estate. It was restored by the National Trust and volunteers in 1997. For seven or eight years it was used on occasional weekends, but is now disused.

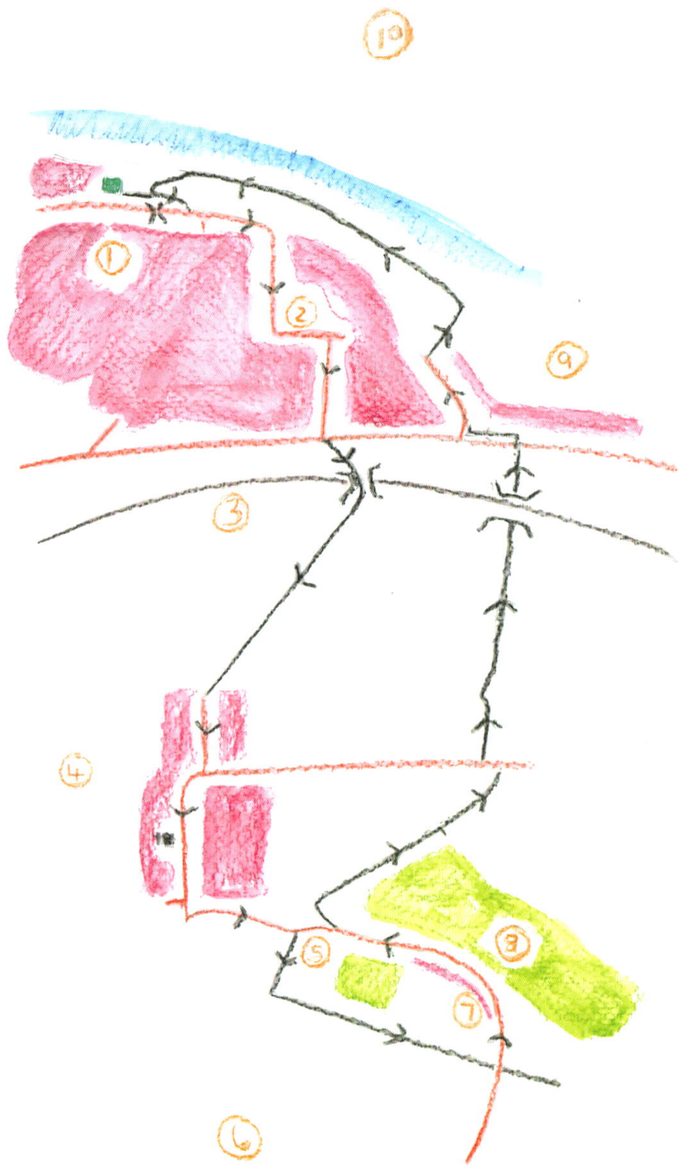
10
1
2
9
3
4
5
8
7
6

Walk 13: *Overstrand, Northrepps and Sidestrand*

Summary

This walk uses public footpaths, tracks and paved footways, there are some gentle and two very steep gradients and uneven ground. It starts from a cliff top car park in Overstrand, with sea views, before heading into Overstrand village, then crosses the main coast road and climbs, through open countryside, to the village of Northrepps and the small hamlet of Frogshall, from there it returns to Overstrand.

The Route

Distance: 6 miles.
Time: 2½/3 hours.
Suggested car park: North Norfolk District Council Car Park, Pauls Lane, Overstrand. NR27 0PE
TG 2462 4110
Map Sheet: OS Explorer 252

1. Leave the car park and follow the path towards the beach access slope, passing the slope, follow the road and turn right into Cliff Road.

2. Continue along Cliff Road until you reach the High Street.

3. Turn left onto the High Street passing Sea Marge Hotel, then turn right into Carr Lane.

4. Follow Carr Lane until you reach the junction.

5. Cross the road with care and follow the track straight ahead (signed Radio Station).

6. Follow the track as it ascends and then descends into Northrepps. You will walk over a bridge crossing a disused railway line. If you look back the way you have just come, there are sea views.

7. At the end of the track, go left into Keswick Close. Ignore the footpath to the right.

8. At the junction, turn right and follow the road, passing the school and parish church. Ignore the footpath to the right.

9. Continue along this road until you reach a staggered crossroads, turn left into Rectory Road.

10. Continue along this road until you reach a sharp left hand bend with a track to the right.

11. Turn right, follow this track (signed Paston Way) passing the Rectory. Ignoring the path to the left, go right and follow the footpath through the hedge (signed Paston Way). From here, there are distant views of Southrepps church.

12. Continue along this path to Frogshall. At the road, turn left passing Frogshall Farmhouse.

13. Continue along this road. Ignore the roadway to the right (signed Templewood) and the footpath to the right.

14. Take the next track to the right (signed Paston Way). As it leaves the woodland edge, follow the path along the field edge, then go left and follow the path, passing the ponds.

15. Continue towards Hungry Hill. Take care when passing the barns as this is a working farm, continue to the road.

16. At the road, turn left and walk for a short distance before turning right onto the bridleway (signed Paston Way).

17. Before you reach the mast, turn left and follow the footpath through the hedge (signed Paston Way). Continue along this path, passing under the bridge, until you reach the road.

18. Cross the road with care, turn left, then right into Coast Road.

19. After a short distance, turn left into Clifton Way. Due to cliff erosion it is not possible to continue along the road and cliff path. Cross the grassed area and descend the steep slope to the beach.

20. Turn left and walk along the promenade, passing the beach huts.

21. Ascend the steep slope, at the top turn right and follow the path back to the car park.

Points of Interest

1. Overstrand

The village of Overstrand has a long history of settlement, with evidence of human occupation dating back to the Palaeolithic period. It was mentioned in the Domesday Book of 1086. The origin of the name Overstrand is obscure. 'Strand' is Old English meaning shore, but the meaning of 'Over' is unclear - it could mean 'other' to distinguish it from Sidestrand or 'narrow shore with a steep edge'.

The oldest building in the village is St Martin's church, which replaced an earlier church washed away in 1399. It was restored in the eighteenth century and again in 1911-1914. The church has a memorial to Sir Thomas Fowell Buxton (1786-1845), brewer, Abolitionist and social reformer.

During the late nineteenth century the area became a popular holiday destination, partly as a consequence of writings of Clement Scott (1841 -1908), theatre critic for the Daily Telegraph, who referred to it as 'Poppyland'. Around the turn of the nineteenth century, a number of fashionable houses were built in the village. Across the road from the car park (behind the brick wall) is The Pleasaunce, adapted from two existing villas between 1897 and 1899 by Sir Edwin Lutyens (1869-1944) (famous as a designer of New Delhi), for Cyril Flower, 1st Baron Battersea (1843-1907) and his wife Constance de Rothschild (1843-1931). Lady Battersea antagonised Lutyens by constantly amending the design of the house and by refusing to agree to the demolition of the original houses. As a consequence, the resulting house is irregular in plan.

Overstrand Hall, built 1900 for Charles Mills (1855-1919), 2nd Baron Hillingdon, was also designed by Lutyens. It is regarded as one of his more over the top designs, it was built in a mixture of materials and styles.

Overstrand has one of the oldest road traffic signs still surviving in the country. Under the 1903 Motor Car Act, local authorities were allowed to erect signs to manage traffic, before the creation of the Ministry of Transport. The road traffic prohibition sign (the equivalent of today's 'No Entry' sign) was erected on the Coast Road between 1904 and 1919 and it remains in its original location. The sign has decoration and detailing not found on later versions.

2. Sea Marge Hotel

Sea Marge, a half-timbered building of two and three storeys, was built between 1908 and 1912, by Sir A.W. Blomfield and Sons, for Sir Edgar Speyer (1862-1932), an American born (of German descent) financier and philanthropist, chairman of Speyer Brothers bank and a director of the German and American branches of the bank. He was naturalised as a British citizen in 1892. He largely financed the Promenade Concerts between 1902 and 1914, and was treasurer for Scott's Antarctic Expedition. He was made a Baronet in 1906 and a Privy Counsellor in 1909. As chairman of Underground Electric Railways Company of London, from 1905, he was responsible for the three deep tubes which form the central sections of today's Bakerloo, Northern and Piccadilly lines. During World War I, he was the subject of a hate campaign (due to his German parentage) and was accused of pro-German activities. One accusation was that he signalled to German submarines from his Overstrand home. Many of these accusations may have had a political motive. An investigation, in 1921, found he had been involved in activities incompatible with his status as a British citizen, something which he always denied. His naturalisation was revoked and he was removed from the list of the privy council. Speyer Brothers was dissolved in 1922 and Speyer left Britain in the early 1920s and returned to the USA. He died in Berlin in 1932. Sea Marge was sold after Speyer's death; it became a hotel in 1935, from 1955 to 1990 it was a care home for the elderly and re-opened as a hotel in 1996. It has been suggested that John Buchan, in his novel 'The Thirty Nine Steps', based the villainous stockbroker, Appleton, on Edgar Speyer.

3. Methodist Chapel, Cliff Road

The Methodist Chapel was designed by Sir Edwin Lutyens, on land given by Lord and Lady Battersea. It opened in 1898. It is said, Lutyen based his design on a boat shed in Littlehampton; however it also has a passing resemblance to a former lifeboat house at Cromer.

4. Norfolk and Suffolk Joint Railway

The railway between North Walsham and Cromer, via Mundesley, was the northern section of the Norfolk and Suffolk Joint Railway (the southern section ran from Gorleston to Lowestoft). The line between Mundesley and Cromer opened in August 1906 and closed in 1953. A small section (around Cromer) is still in use as part of the Bittern Line from Norwich to Sheringham. Other sections of the track bed have been turned into footpaths. Overstrand railway station was converted into a house.

5. Northrepps

There is limited evidence for human activity in the prehistoric, Roman or Saxon periods in Northrepps. In the Domesday Book of 1086, the parish is said to be of little value, but it records there were two mills and a church. The name Northrepps derived from the Old English word 'repel' which means strips of land in a fen that could be tilled. In 1906, the parish was reduced in size, losing land to Overstrand. The parish is made up of the village of Northrepps and the hamlets of Frogshall and Crossdale Street.

Northrepps Foundry was an ironfounders, smithy and wheelwrights which operated from 1820 to 1938. Between 1999 and 2000 the site was converted for housing. Northrepps school was built in 1870.

6. St Mary's Church, Northrepps

St Mary's church dates from the late fourteenth/early fifteenth century and was significantly restored in the nineteenth century. It has the remains of a perpendicular style rood screen and in the south aisle twentieth century stained glass, depicting a host of angels.

7. The Rectory

The Rectory, an impressive building, was built about 1815 and is rectangular in plan, with a central portico with fluted Doric columns and pilasters and overhanging eaves.

8. St James' Church, Southrepps

St James' church has one of the tallest towers in Norfolk and dates to the mid fifteenth century. The aisles were demolished in 1791, and the arcades infilled to form the nave walls. Parts of the church were restored in the nineteenth century. It has a collection of late nineteenth and early twentieth century stained glass.

9. Frogshall Farmhouse

Frogshall Farmhouse dates from the eighteenth century but was built around an earlier core.

10. Templewood

Just visible through the trees is Templewood, a 'shooting box' used as a base for country pursuits, which incorporates architectural fragments from Northhall Temple, Nottinghamshire and the Old Bank of England, London. It was completed in 1938 for Sir Samuel Hoare, Viscount Templewood, by the architect John Seely (1899-1963) and Paul Paget (1901-1985). The house is set in 80 hectares (200 acres) of woodland, which originally included grassed areas and water.

11. Sidestrand

Sidestrand is another long established settlement, a hand axe dating to the Palaeolithic was found on the beach and there is evidence of what could possibly be Iron Age or Roman field systems in the parish. It was mentioned in the Domesday Book Of 1086. The name Sidestrand derives from Old English meaning 'wide shore'. The parish has been subject to extensive coastal erosion. The site of the old St Michael's church lies to the north east of the present building. It was demolished in 1880, because of the threat of cliff loss. Much of the medieval material was used to build the present church in 1881, the tower is a copy of the original. The tower of old St Michael's was left and remained standing until 1916, the last part of the old churchyard fell into the sea in 1936. The churchyard was the setting for Clement Scott's poem 'Garden of Sleep'.

12. Doggerland

As you stand on the cliff top and look out to sea you are looking at what was once Doggerland - a swampy plain stretching to The Netherlands, Denmark and Norway. Until 12,000 years ago, it would have been possible for hunter gathers to live and roam across much of the area of what is now the North Sea.

Notes about walk

Walk 14: *Mundesley, Bacton, Edingthorpe, (Paston) & Knapton*

Summary

This walk uses footpaths, bridleways and country lanes, there are one or two moderate gradients and some walking along the foreshore. Leaving the beach at Bacton it climbs through arable fields to Bacton church, and then on to Edingthorpe and Knapton from where descends into Mundesley with views back to Bacton. There is a detour to Paston, which can be turned into an alternative route, for those who would like to explore two buildings (the church and Great Barn) associated with the Paston family.

The Route

Distance: 9 miles.
Time: 3/3½ hours.
Suggested car park: North Norfolk District Council Car Park, Beach Road / Gold Park, Mundesley. NRll 8BG
TG 3134 3662
Map Sheet: OS Explorer 252
Alternative car parking: Car park, Edingthorpe church

1. Leave the car park and turn right onto Beach Road, follow the road, passing The Ship Inn. Take care on the narrow section where there are no pavements and a sharp bend to the left.

2. At the top of the hill, go through the gate and descend the slope to the beach. (Mundesley Inshore Lifeboat Station is to your left).

3. Head eastwards (right) along the beach towards Bacton. In the distance you can see the tall tower of Happisburgh church. Check the state of the tide and kept to the damp sand for the easiest walking.

4. After approximately 2¼ miles (the sight of Bacton Gas Terminal on the cliff top will indicate you are near the end of the beach walk), turn right, leaving the beach by the slipway (signed Paston Way).

5. Turn left and follow the path, then go right over the 'hump-back' and walk along Kimberley Road (signed Paston Way).

6. At the road junction, cross the road with care and go right and follow the footpath along the field edge as it climbs towards Bacton church (signed Paston Way).

7. Walk through the churchyard, then go right and follow the path to the road.

8. At the road, turn right and walk to the junction. If you wish to visit Paston follow the directions in the alternative route*.

9. Continue straight ahead for about ¾ mile, (signed Edingthorpe).

10. When you reach Edingthorpe, turn right and follow the farm track (between two residential properties and signed Paston Way), as it climbs through the farmyard towards the church.

11. At the copse, turn left and follow the path along the edge of the churchyard.

12. Continue along the path as it descends from the church car park. At the bottom, turn right and follow the path for a short distance.

13. Then go left and follow the path across the field.

14. Go through the hedge, turn left and follow the path along the field edge.

15. Go through the hedge and turn right onto the road. Follow this road as it bends to the left and then to the right.

16. Just after the right hand bend, turn left and follow the footpath across the field.

17. Go through the hedge and follow the path across the field towards the building (former Paston and Knapton Railway Station).

18. Keep the building to your right, follow the path over the footbridge (crossing a disused railway), then cross the field towards Knapton.

19. Follow the path as it weaves its way between the houses to reach the road.

20. At the road, turn left and continue towards the church.

21. Both routes: turn right at the churchyard, into Pond Lane.

22. Follow this road to its junction with the B1145. There are distant views towards Bacton from this road.

23. Cross the B1145 with care, turning right, and walk along the verge for a short distance. Follow the path over the bank into the field and continue along the field edge.

24. On leaving the path, take care when walking the last few metres to the junction, the verges are high and there is no footway.

25. At the junction, turn left and then right into the High Street.

26. Where the road forks, take the right fork and walk until you reach the entrance to Gold Park.

27. Go into the park and follow the path back to the car park.

* Alternative Route

1. Turn right at the junction and follow the road towards Paston.

2. At the junction, turn left and walk to the church and the Great Barn.

3. After visiting the church and the Great Barn, you can either return to the main walk by retracing your steps or turn left and walk to the first junction after the Great Barn, then turn left.

4. Follow this road for approximately ½ mile (ignore the road to the right) until you reach a fork in the road. Take the road to the right and follow the road under the bridge and head towards Knapton village.

5. At the church follow the direction given in the main route (21).

Points of Interest

1. Mundesley

Mundesley is a small seaside town with a long history, the earliest archaeological finds date to the Palaeothic period and there is evidence of a Roman Road. Its name derives from Old English meaning 'Mundel's clearing'. It is mentioned in the Domesday Book of 1086. One the oldest building in Mundesley is All Saints' church which was originally built in the fourteenth and fifteenth centuries. It was completely rebuilt between 1899-1914, using material from the old church. The rood screen dates from the restoration, but the pulpit with tester is Jacobean and the font dates from the fourteenth century.

Mundesley Holiday Camp, opened in 1933, was the first purpose built fully catered holiday camp in Norfolk and only the second to be built in Britain. Its layout was intended to mirror the sails of the Stow Mill. During World War II it was used as a military training camp.

Stow Mill, situated on the edge of Mundesley, is actually in the parish of Paston. It is a four storey tarred brick tower mill built in 1827, by James Gaze, and continued working until 1930. Until 2014, it was open to the public, but has since been converted to a holiday let.

The name 'stow' means a resting place, it is said there was a medieval chapel here which provided pilgrims travelling between Bromholm and Walsingham with a place to rest.

2. The Dell, 14 Beach Road

The Dell, 14 Beach Road is an early nineteenth century cottage in the Gothick style.

3. Water Wheel

The water wheel and the mill pond above are now all that remains of Mundesley Watermill, which was built about 1723. It had five floors (but from the footpath by the mill pond, it would have appeared to have only two, the mill pond was level with the third floor) and an overshot water wheel. It was worked by the Larter family until the 1920s. In addition to grinding grain it was used to provide electricity to some of the surrounding properties. The mill burned down in 1956, although the shell of the building was not demolished until 1965. The water from the pond flows under the road and out into the North Sea.

4. Bacton

The earliest evidence for human settlement in Bacton comes from Neolithic finds found at Bacton Wood Farm. The name Bacton derives from Old English meaning 'Bacca's enclosure'. To the north of Bacton was the settlement of Keswick. The church at Keswick, St Clement's, was at risk from coastal erosion in 1386, its foundations were finally washed away in 1760. Today the parish of Bacton is made up of the village of Bacton and the small hamlets of Keswick, Pollard Street, Bacton Green and, since 1935, Edingthorpe.

The mound of sand in front of the cliffs at Bacton Gas Terminal forms part of a 'sandscaping' scheme carried out in 2018. 1.8 million tonnes of sand were pumped onto the beach, widening it and creating a gentle slope, which is designed to protect the cliffs at the gas terminal from erosion and the villages of Bacton and Walcott from flooding.

Not far from the route there was once a terminal hut for the Borkum to Bacton submarine telegraph cable. From Bacton the cable ran overhead to North Walsham. The hut and telegraph poles were still in existence until the 1990s; a house now occupies the site.

The village has a Type K6 telephone box designed, in 1935, by Sir Giles Gilbert Scott (1880-1960).

During the medieval period Bacton had a very important pilgrimage site. Bromholm Priory, a Cluniac house dedicated to St Andrew, was founded in 1113 by William de Glanville. Until 1298, it was a subordinate to the priory at Castle Acre. Bromholm Priory became a national pilgrimage site after it acquired a fragment of the True Cross; reputedly from a chaplain who had fled Constantinople in 1204. According to the Benedictine monk and chronicler, Matthew Paris, the chaplain had offered the relic to a number of other monasteries, but all had declined it. Paris describes

Bromholm as being very poor at the time of this acquisition. The first miracle associated with the relic was said to have taken place in 1223. The shine became fashionable and was patronised by Henry III and Edward II. It remained popular until it was dissolved in 1536. The priory was mentioned by Chaucer in 'The Canterbury Tales' and by Langton in 'The Vision of Piers Plowman'. In 1466, Sir John Paston, who died in London, was brought to Bromholm for burial. The Pastons were great patrons of the Priory. After dissolution, the site was granted to Robert Southwell, solicitor to the Court of Augmentations. Little is known of its history from this point onwards. There is some evidence it was used for commercial purposes, perhaps as a market. In the 1830s, it was used as a 'quarry' for agricultural buildings by Colonel Wodehouse, who then owned the site. A number of houses in the village have reused stone from the priory. Remains of the north transept, chapter house, part of the dormitory and two gate houses are still standing in the grounds of Abbey Farm.

5. St Andrew's Church, Bacton

St Andrew's church is in part Norman, but mostly dates from the fourteenth century and was remodelled in the fifteenth century. It was restored in 1847. The four stage tower can be dated by bequests of 1459-1485. It has a fourteenth century font and sixteenth century wall paintings. In the churchyard, is a listed Art Nouveau memorial to the Montgomery family.

6. The Vicarage, Bacton

The Vicarage has a facade which dates to about 1780, with an earlier house to the rear. It is now a private house.

Bacton Vicarage was the childhood home of the composer Ernest John Moeran (1894-1950). His father, the Reverend Joseph Moeran, served in a number of parishes in Norfolk including Bacton. As a young man, E. J. Moeran collected folk tunes from public houses around North-East Norfolk.

7. Edingthorpe

All Saints' church, Edingthorpe, dates back to the late Saxon or early Norman period. The tower and nave date to the twentieth century and the chancel is fourteenth century, with later alterations. The fourteenth century octagonal belfry can be dated by a tower bequest of 1375. It has a fourteenth century decorated font and rare fourteenth century wall paintings on the north wall and a nineteenth century kingpost chancel roof.

The poet Siegfried Sassoon stayed at the Old Rectory, as a child, with his parents and siblings. He returned in 1937 and mentions Edingthorpe in his memoirs.

8. Paston

The earliest datable archaeological finds found in Paston are Neolithic axe heads. Its name derives from Old English meaning 'enclosure by the small pools'. The oldest surviving building in the village is St Margaret's

church which dates to the fourteenth century, but is on the site of an earlier building. It is a comparatively simple building given its association with the wealthy Paston family; however Bromholm Priory was still in existence when the family was at the height of their fame and fortune. The most senior members of the family chose to be buried and spent their money there, rather than at St Margaret's. There are some memorials to the Pastons in the church. In the 1920s, wall paintings were discovered on the north wall.

The Great Barn next to the church is attributed to Sir William Paston and was built in 1581. The roof is alternating hammer beam and tie beam trusses; the span of the roof does not require the use of hammer beams, so they were probably used as a display of wealth. There were plans to turn the barn into a visitor centre, but these were abandoned because of the presence of rare bats.

Paston Hall, which is on the site of a hall once owned by the Paston family, dates from the mid-nineteenth century.

The Paston family is famous today because of the letters they wrote in the fifteenth century, during the Wars of the Roses. The family was 100 years in establishing their wealth and influence, 100 years at the height of that wealth and influence and 100 years in decline. The first recorded Paston was Clement, a yeoman farmer from Paston, who died in 1419. His son, William, trained as a lawyer, eventually becoming a judge, and began the family's rise. William's son John also trained as a lawyer and was an executor to the will of Sir John Fastoff, of Caister Castle, the inspiration for Shakespeare's Falstaff. John Paston acquired property from Fastoff's will. The family built two houses in Norfolk, Oxnead Hall and Barningham Hall, and founded a free school (later a grammar school and now a sixth form college) at North Walsham. Twice the family was on the wrong side of events and this was the ultimate cause of their decline. They were Royalists in the Parliamentary county of Norfolk and at the end of the Civil War, their estate was sequestered by the government of Cromwell. At the Restoration of Charles II, Robert Paston (1631-1683) was created 1st Earl of Yarmouth as a reward for the family's loyalty. Having converted to Catholicism in 1687, William Paston (1654-1732), 2nd Earl of Yarmouth, was made Treasurer to the Household by James II. Although he reconverted to Anglicanism in 1689, he refused to swear allegiance to William III and Mary II and suffered loss of office and was twice imprisoned on suspicion of Jacobitism. The family's fortunes did not recover from these events. The 2nd Earl of Yarmouth, the last of the Pastons, spent much of his life trying to keep one step ahead of bankruptcy. When he died in 1732, his daughter (three sons had predeceased him) decided the debts were so great there was no option but to sell Oxnead Hall and its contents.

The large barn, opposite the Great Barn, was built in 1936/7 by the East Anglian Real Property Company, owned by Dutch nationals, and was one of twelve barns they built in East Anglia, for the storage of sugar beet. All were painted red and were next to large fields, created by the removal of obstructions such as hedges and ditches.

9. Paston and Knapton Railway Station

Paston and Knapton Railway Station was on the Norfolk and Suffolk Joint Railway (Northern Section) line from Cromer Beach to North Walsham. The station was opened in 1898 and served the villages of Paston and Knapton. It closed in 1964. It has been converted into a house.

10. Knapton

Knapton is a small village with a long history. The earliest archaeological evidence of human activity in the area are Neolithic flint axe heads. The name Knapton is derived from Old English and means 'Cnapa's settlement or farm'.

It is mentioned in the Domesday Book of 1086 as 'Kanapatone'. The village was the birthplace of Walter Pardon (1914-1996), carpenter and traditional folk singer. Knapton Hall dates from about 1800 and is now an hotel.

11. St Peter's and St Paul's Church

St Peter's and St. Paul's church is mainly fourteenth century, with fifteenth century remodelling and was restored in 1882 by George Gilbert Scott (1839-1897). It has a very interesting double hammer beam roof, seventy feet in length and over thirty feet wide with carved figures (most decapitated) and painted angels (which date to 1882, all other details date to 1504). It has a thirteenth century font (with a Greek inscription, which reads in translation 'Wash thou, not only my face, but my transgression') with a timber font cover dating to 1704 and a partly restored fifteenth century rood screen. The pulpit appears to be eighteenth century, but dates to the nineteenth century restoration. The weather vane which tops the tower was modelled on a drawing by the Norwich artist John Sell Cotman (1784-1842).

Notes about walk

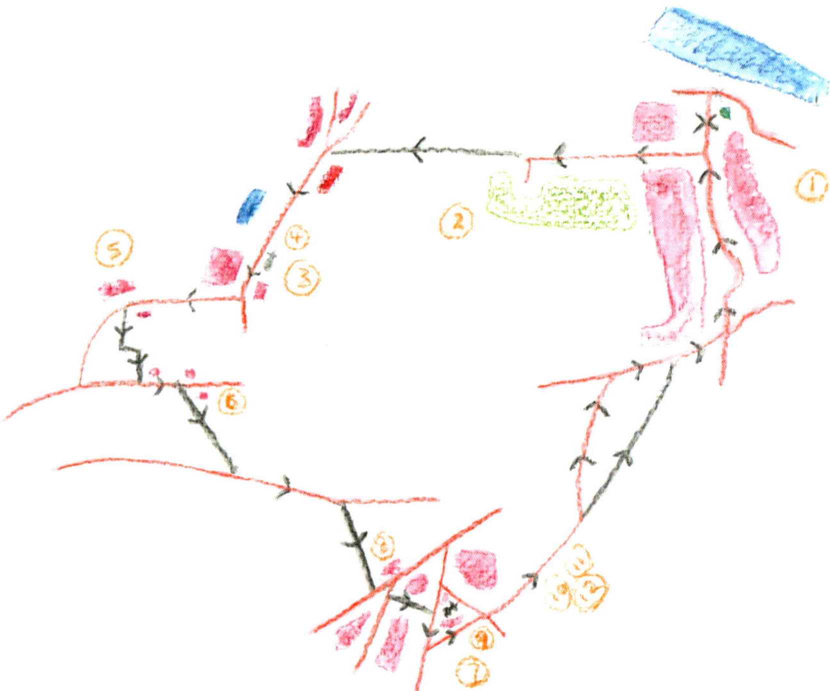
1
2
3
4
5
6
7
8
9

Walk 15: *Mundesley, Gimingham and Trunch*

Summary

This walk uses public footpaths, byways as well as country lanes and urban roads. There are some inclines and uneven ground. It begins in the small seaside town of Mundesley and then descends through arable fields to Gimingham and on to Trunch before returning to Mundesley.

The Route

Distance: 7¼ miles.
Time: 3/3½ hours.
Suggested car park: North Norfolk District Council Car Park, Beach Road, Gold Park, Mundesley. NRll 8BG
TG 3134 3662
Map Sheet: OS Explorer 252
Alternative car parking: Shoppers Car Park, Station Road, Mundesley

1. Leave the car park and turn left onto Beach Road.

2. After a short distance, turn left into High Street.

3. Turn right into Station Road. Follow this road for a short distance, then

4. Turn left into Links Road. Continue along this road with Mundesley Golf Course to the left. There are views of the sea, the old Continental Hotel and Mundesley and Trimingham from this road.

5. The road ends with a sharp turn to the left. Before the entrance to the golf course, turn right, go through the hedge and follow the footpath (signed Paston Way/public footpath/circular walk), with Mundesley Golf Course to your left. Here there are distant views of Trunch church.

6. At the end of the golf course, follow the footpath straight ahead, crossing the arable field (signed Paston Way), there are distant views of Southrepps church.

7. Go through the hedge (signed Paston Way) and follow the path as it begins to climb, keep the hedge to your left.

8. Go through the gate and follow the path, keeping the hedge to your left.

9. Go through the gate and follow the path across the field, heading towards Gimingham.

10. At the field edge, go through the opening and walk between the houses to the road.

11. At the road, turn left (Mill Street) and follow this road, passing the mill ponds, into Church Street.

12. Continue along the road, passing All Saints' church on your left, until you reach the village sign/hall.

13. At the village sign, turn right (Hall Road). Follow this road until you reach Hall Farm.

14. Ignoring the path to the right, follow the road around a sharp left bend. Just beyond Barn 3, go left and follow the footpath (signed circular walk/ public footpath/church walk).

15. At the end of the garden, go right and follow the path into the field.

16. At the end of the field turn left and after a short distance, turn right and walk towards the houses. The path passes close to the wall of Dial Lodge.

17. At the road turn left, (ignore the footpath to the right) and follow the road to Robin Cottage/Royal Farm, then

18. Turn right and follow the wide track, passing a pond on the right and continue to the road.

19. At the road, turn left (signed Paston Way/Trunch Mundesley Circular walk). Follow the road towards Trunch.

20. Follow the road as it bends to the right, then immediately after the bend turn right and follow the footpath (signed circular walk/public footpath/ byway/church link) into Trunch. There are distant views of Bradfield church.

21. At the road turn left and walk to the junction (Wright's Lane).

22. Turn right into Wright's Lane, then immediately left and follow the footpath between the garden fences towards St Botolph's church (signed circular walk/church link/Paston Way).

23. At the end of the path, turn right and walk to the village sign.

24. At the village sign, cross the road, turn left, keeping the church to your left.

25. At the junction, go right and then take the road to the left (signed Mundesley 2¼ miles). Walk by Trunch Town Pump.

26. Continue along this road passing several large farmhouses. There are distant views of Knapton church.

27. Continue along this road towards Mundesley. The sails of Stow Mill, Paston are just visible above the trees. The footpath along this road can be used to walk back to Mundesley - see alternative route below.

An alternative route: At the footpath sign, turn right and cross the field towards the far corner. Go through the hedge and follow the path to the plank bridge. Cross the footbridge, going through the hedge, and follow the path across the field towards the houses. At the road turn right and join the main route. (29)

28. At the junction (by Tree House Farm), turn right and follow the road into Mundesley. As the route passes the school it is joined by the alternative route.

29. Both routes: follow the road towards the village centre, ignore the road to the right (signed Knapton/North Walsham), cross the bridge over Mundesley Beck/River Mun.

30. Continue along High Street to the fork in the road, take the right fork and head towards the village sign.

31. At the village sign turn right into the park and follow the path back to the car park.

Points of Interest

1. Mundesley

Also see Points of Interest to Walk 14.

Mundesley Railway Station was on the North Walsham to Cromer line and opened in August 1906, the line from Cromer to Mundesley closed in 1953 and North Walsham to Mundesley in 1964. In an attempt to encourage visitors to use the railway, the London and North Eastern Railway (LNER), like many railway companies, introduced camping coaches to selected stations. These were old coaches no longer in service, which had been adapted to provide living and sleeping space. Mundesley Station had one camping coach in 1938-39, four in 1952, eleven in 1953-58, then ten in 1959 reduced to six in 1960-64. Three remained in 1965, despite the fact the station had closed a year earlier. Nothing remains of the station today, the site was redeveloped for housing.

At the end of the nineteenth century there was an attempt to develop the North Norfolk coast as a fashionable holiday destination. Three large hotels were built in Mundesley; the Clarence Hotel in 1891, it closed in 1938 and became a nursing home, the Grand Hotel in 1897 and the Manor Hotel (designed by Norwich architect John Bond Pearce (1843-1903) in 1900. The Grand Hotel, standing high on the cliff top, is a dominant landmark. During World War II it was requisitioned for military use, returning to private ownership after the war with a new name, Continental Hotel. It was later closed and converted into flats.

The poet and author William Cowper (1731-1800) spent time in Mundesley 1795-96, he found the air suited his 'melancholia'.

2. Mundesley Hospital

Mundesley Hospital (actually in the parish of Gimingham) was the first large tuberculosis sanatorium to be built in Britain. It was built in 1898/9 by Boulton and Paul of Norwich, for Dr F. W. Burton-Fanning (1863-1937). Having worked at Addenbrookes, Burton-Fanning was elected a physician at the Norfolk and Norwich Hospital in 1891. During frequent visits to Davos, Switzerland, he became interested in open-air treatment for pulmonary tuberculosis. In 1895, he began to put this treatment into practice at Cromer Convalescent Hospital, later opening, with his cousin, W.J. Fanning, Mundesley Sanatorium for private patients. Mundesley was modelled on sanatoria in Germany and Switzerland. It is a prefabricated timber-framed building with an iron roof. Boulton and Paul later marketed it as a standard design for their sanitoria. It became a hospital in 1957 and closed in 1992. Since then the building has been used by various

private clinics. Dr Burton-Fanning added Mundesley Golf Course in 1901, to provide his wealthy patients with the opportunity for exercise. The course was designed by the six times Open winner, Harry Vardon (1870-1937). In 1903, Vardon contracted tuberculosis and went for treatment at Mundesley Hospital.

In 1903, Dr Burton-Fanning opened Kelling Sanatorium for non-paying patients. He retired from the Norfolk and Norwich Hospital in 1928, but continued to practice for the remainder of his life.

3. Gimingham

Gimingham has a long settlement history. The earliest datable archaeological finds are from the Neolithic period. Its name is Old English meaning 'the homestead of the family or followers of Gymi or Gymma'. It is mentioned in the Domesday Book of 1086 as part of a manor that included Knapton and Sidestrand.

All Saints' church dates from the fourteenth century, with the large south porch added in the late fifteenth or early sixteenth century. The tower is fifteenth century. It was restored in the 1860s and the interior is essentially a Victorian church. Some of the old bench ends have been preserved.

4. Gimingham Watermill

Giminingham watermill was originally built in the eighteenth century and had four storeys, two sunk below ground level. The mill

worked until 1976. It was demolished in 1980 following a fire in 1979. A new building was put on the site. The mill was powered by water from the long, zigzag, mill pond.

The Crosley steam engine came from Crisps Maltings at East Dereham and was moved to Gimingham in 1937.

5. Gimingham Hall

Gimingham Hall (Hall farmhouse) is a late seventeenth or early eighteenth century house. To the east of the house was a medieval hall owned by the Duchy of Lancaster, which burned down around 1700.

6. John of Gaunt's House

John of Gaunt's House is a Jacobean brick house with a thatched roof. Despite its name, it is not thought to be the site of his hall. The site of John of Gaunt's hall is thought to be Gimingham Hall.

7. Trunch

Trunch is a village with a long history. There have been archaeological finds from the Mesolithic, Neolithic and Bronze Age found in the area. It is mentioned in the Domesday Book of 1086. The meaning of the name Trunch is unclear. It may refer to the fact that the Le Tronchet Abbey had possessions in the area, or it may derive from Celtic meaning 'woods on a promontory'. In 1581, Robert Thexton became Rector of Trunch. While at Cambridge University, Thexton had shared rooms with the Elizabethan playwright, Christopher Marlowe. Trunch is famous for the Trunchonbury music festival.

8. Manor Farm Barns

Manor Farm barns are a complex of barns one of which dates to the 1590s. There is a twentieth century barn built using nineteenth century material.

9. St Botolph's Church

St Botolph's Church has a most interesting ecclesiastical treasure, an early fifteenth century font canopy. Dating to just before the Reformation it provides a glimpse of the way English Catholic art was developing. Made of oak, silvered with age, it is carved with fruit, flowers, leopards and lions in six octagonal columns. The niches at the top are large enough to hold multiple figures. The church has a fifteenth century hammer beam roof and a rood screen dating to 1502, painted with representations of the Apostles and St Paul.

10. Ivy Farmhouse

Ivy Farmhouse is a seventeenth century house with a Georgian front. One of the two barns dates to 1727, the other is late eighteenth century.

11. Brick Kiln Farmhouse

Brick Kiln Farmhouse is a seventeenth century house remodelled in the eighteenth and nineteenth centuries.

12. Hall Farmhouse

Hall Farmhouse is a late sixteenth century house with two sixteenth century barns.